Application Development in iOS 7

Learn how to build an entire real-world application using all of iOS 7's new features

Kyle Begeman

PUBLISHING

BIRMINGHAM - MUMBAI

Application Development in iOS 7

Copyright © 2014 Packt Publishing

First published: May 2014

Production Reference: 1120514

Published by Packt Publishing Ltd.
Livery Place
35 Livery Street
Birmingham B3 2PB, UK.

ISBN 978-1-78355-031-9

www.packtpub.com

Cover Image by Pratyush Mohanta (tysoncinematography@gmail.com)

Credits

Author
Kyle Begeman

Reviewers
Arnaud Coomans
Jayant C. Varma
Dmitry Volevodz

Commissioning Editor
James Jones

Acquisition Editor
James Jones

Content Development Editor
Rikshith Shetty

Technical Editors
Pramod Kumavat
Mukul Pawar

Copy Editors
Sarang Chari
Adithi Shetty

Project Coordinator
Harshal Ved

Proofreaders
Stephen Copestake
Maria Gould
Paul Hindle

Indexer
Mehreen Deshmukh

Graphics
Yuvraj Mannari

Production Coordinators
Kyle Albuquerque
Conidon Miranda

Cover Work
Conidon Miranda

About the Author

Kyle Begeman is a self-taught programmer, entrepreneur, and educator. With over five years of experience in iOS development, he has produced multiple applications, mostly with large businesses. He frequently produces educational videos and text for others to learn how to program. A self-proclaimed nerd living in the Silicon Valley, Kyle Begeman spends most of his free time listening to/playing music and thinking up the next great project! You can visit his website at www.kylebegeman.com.

For my wife, Kelli. You inspire me every day on our journey through life.

About the Reviewers

Arnaud Coomans is a senior iOS engineer. He has developed various applications, both for iPhone and iPad, and regularly contributes to open source projects. He enjoys reverse engineering, writing libraries, and writing Xcode plugins.

After working for different startups, including his own, Arnaud Coomans is now working on mobile applications for one of the biggest companies in Silicon Valley.

> I would like to thank my family and friends for their help
> and support.

Jayant C. Varma is an Australian author, developer trainer, and consultant with a special focus on mobile development and the use of mobile applications in business. He is the author of the book *Learn Lua for iOS Game Development, Apress,* and is the Principal Consultant at OZ Apps, a company he founded, specializing in mobile business solutions.

He has been in the IT industry for quite a while and has seen things change from 8-bit computers to 64-bit mobile devices. He has been drawn towards new technology and Usable UI (user friendly and appealing). He has had several roles earlier that have seen him in different countries as the IT Manager for BMW dealerships working on wireless diagnostics and contactless key readers, among other things, to lecturing at the James Cook University and being actively involved with training and workshops for the Apple University Consortium (AUC) and Australian Computer Society (ACS). Among the well-known apps that he, as a developer, has created is the text-based adventure, *Z-Day Survival Simulator* application.

He has been a reviewer on a couple of Packt Publishing books based on iOS usage and development. He runs a few blogs on development, such as `http://howto.oz-apps.com` and `http://LearnLua.oz-apps.com`, among others.

Dmitry Volevodz is an experienced iOS developer. He has been doing freelance software development for a few years, but has now settled in a small company. He does enterprise iOS development, and game development is his hobby. He has written *iOS 7 Game Development, Packt Publishing*, a title about game development with Sprite Kit.

I thank my wife Olesya for her patience and my son.

www.PacktPub.com

Support files, eBooks, discount offers, and more

You might want to visit www.PacktPub.com for support files and downloads related to your book.

Did you know that Packt offers eBook versions of every book published, with PDF and ePub files available? You can upgrade to the eBook version at www.PacktPub.com and as a print book customer, you are entitled to a discount on the eBook copy. Get in touch with us at service@packtpub.com for more details.

At www.PacktPub.com, you can also read a collection of free technical articles, sign up for a range of free newsletters, and receive exclusive discounts and offers on Packt books and eBooks.

http://PacktLib.PacktPub.com

Do you need instant solutions to your IT questions? PacktLib is Packt's online digital book library. Here, you can access, read and search across Packt's entire library of books.

Why subscribe?

- Fully searchable across every book published by Packt
- Copy and paste, print, and bookmark content
- On demand and accessible via web browser

Free access for Packt account holders

If you have an account with Packt at www.PacktPub.com, you can use this to access PacktLib today and view nine entirely free books. Simply use your login credentials for immediate access.

Table of Contents

Preface

Welcome to *Application Development in iOS 7*. With the release of iOS 7, Apple has completely changed the way we developers think about mobile application design and development. In addition to a complete visual overhaul, iOS 7 offers hundreds of new API and SDK improvements as well as a completely revamped development environment, Xcode 5. This book will walk you through a step-by-step process of building a fully functional application from scratch. By the end of this book, you will have a complete understanding of many of the major changes to iOS 7 development and will be ready to start making better applications for your users!

What this book covers

Chapter 1, Xcode 5 – A Developer's Ultimate Tool, explains everything you need to know to get the most out of Apple's IDE. With the new Xcode, developing and managing applications has never been easier.

Chapter 2, Foundation Framework – Growing Up, introduces the Foundation framework, as it is one of the most important and core frameworks in all of iOS development. When Apple makes changes to it, you want to pay attention!

Chapter 3, Auto Layout 2.0, explains the implementation of Auto Layout 2.0 in iOS 7. When Auto Layout was first introduced, it contained multiple problems that caused many developers to avoid using it. With iOS 7, Apple heeded these concerns and made many of the required improvements.

Chapter 4, Building Our Application for iOS 7, guides us to build our own application as we now know the ins and outs of Xcode 5, the Foundation framework, and the new Auto Layout. We will start our first project and focus on the new iOS 7 design principles.

Chapter 5, Creating and Saving User Data, enables us to prepare an application to support users in creating new items and saving the data for later use. For example, in our custom application, users will be able to save the food they eat to view later on.

Chapter 6, Displaying User Data, explains the technique to display the data that we have saved. This is the final step that completes our application before we move on to two major iOS 7 APIs.

Chapter 7, Manipulating Text with TextKit, explains the use of TextKit, a new API in iOS 7, which streamlines the process of working with text. From dynamic type to rich text editor styles, TextKit is an excellent tool for any iOS developer to understand.

Chapter 8, Adding Physics with UIKit Dynamics, explains the use of UIKit Dynamics, which is a fully featured physics engine built directly into UIKit. UIKit Dynamics will allow you to create physics-based movement and animations in your application for a real-world feel.

What you need for this book

You will need the following for this book:

- Apple computer running OS X 10.8 or higher
- Xcode 5 installed on your Mac

Who this book is for

This book is for iOS developers looking to learn the new features of iOS 7 and Xcode 5. A basic understanding of Objective-C and the iOS SDK is required to properly understand the content of this book.

Conventions

In this book, you will find a number of styles of text that distinguish between different kinds of information. Here are some examples of these styles, and an explanation of their meaning.

Code words in text, database table names, folder names, filenames, file extensions, pathnames, dummy URLs, user input, and Twitter handles are shown as follows: "iOS 7 introduces a completely new class to the Foundation framework, NSProgress."

A block of code is set as follows:

```
-  (void)preferredContentSizeChanged:(NSNotification *)notification {
      self.textView.font = [UIFont preferredFontForTextStyle:UIFontTextS
tyleHeadline];
   }
```

When we wish to draw your attention to a particular part of a code block, the relevant lines or items are set in bold:

```
-  (void)preferredContentSizeChanged:(NSNotification *)notification {
      self.textView.font = [UIFont preferredFontForTextStyle:UIFontTextS
tyleHeadline];
   }
```

New terms and **important words** are shown in bold. Words that you see on the screen, in menus, or dialog boxes for example, appear in the text like this: "Select **Single View Application** and then click on **Next**."

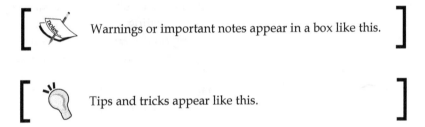

> Warnings or important notes appear in a box like this.

> Tips and tricks appear like this.

Reader feedback

Feedback from our readers is always welcome. Let us know what you think about this book—what you liked or may have disliked. Reader feedback is important for us to develop titles that you really get the most out of.

To send us general feedback, simply send an e-mail to feedback@packtpub.com, and mention the book title via the subject of your message.

If there is a topic that you have expertise in and you are interested in either writing or contributing to a book, see our author guide on www.packtpub.com/authors.

Customer support

Now that you are the proud owner of a Packt book, we have a number of things to help you to get the most from your purchase.

Downloading the example code

You can download the example code files for all Packt books you have purchased from your account at http://www.packtpub.com. If you purchased this book elsewhere, you can visit http://www.packtpub.com/support and register to have the files e-mailed directly to you.

Errata

Although we have taken every care to ensure the accuracy of our content, mistakes do happen. If you find a mistake in one of our books—maybe a mistake in the text or the code—we would be grateful if you would report this to us. By doing so, you can save other readers from frustration and help us improve subsequent versions of this book. If you find any errata, please report them by visiting http://www.packtpub. com/submit-errata, selecting your book, clicking on the **errata submission form** link, and entering the details of your errata. Once your errata are verified, your submission will be accepted and the errata will be uploaded on our website, or added to any list of existing errata, under the Errata section of that title. Any existing errata can be viewed by selecting your title from http://www.packtpub.com/support.

Piracy

Piracy of copyright material on the Internet is an ongoing problem across all media. At Packt, we take the protection of our copyright and licenses very seriously. If you come across any illegal copies of our works, in any form, on the Internet, please provide us with the location address or website name immediately so that we can pursue a remedy.

Please contact us at copyright@packtpub.com with a link to the suspected pirated material.

We appreciate your help in protecting our authors, and our ability to bring you valuable content.

Questions

You can contact us at questions@packtpub.com if you are having a problem with any aspect of the book, and we will do our best to address it.

1
Xcode 5 – A Developer's Ultimate Tool

With the release of iOS 7, Apple has also provided developers with a completely updated version of Xcode, that is, its **Integrated Development Environment (IDE)**. Xcode 5 is a major step forward, complete with more tools and features available than ever before.

Understanding the powerful features of your IDE is the key to high productivity and overall ease of development. In this chapter, we will explore all these new features and learn how they will assist you in writing your apps for iOS 7.

The new user experience

Xcode 5 features many welcomed changes to its overall user experience in the form of subtle design enhancements and under-the-hood optimization. Take a few minutes to play with the new IDE, and you will see that although not much has moved, the cleaner UI provides a much less distracting environment to work in. Shorter toolbars and easy-to-see highlighted buttons help keep your content front and center.

The following screenshot shows how the window of the new IDE looks:

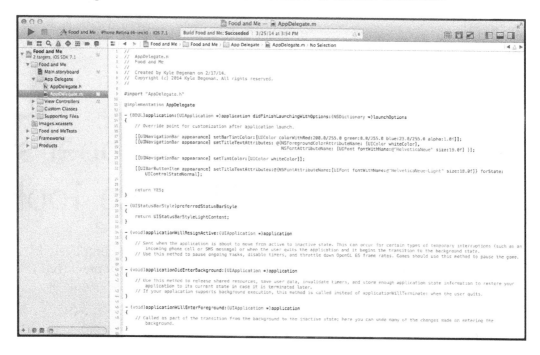

Features such as Open Quickly have been trimmed down in size, yet improved in functionality. Navigating to **File | Open Quickly** or using the keyboard shortcut *command + shift + O* will open a simplified single-line search bar in the middle of your screen. As you type an option, search results are returned much more quickly and prioritized based on relevance. Each result also features detailed data on your query such as the file and line number. The following screenshot shows an example of search results:

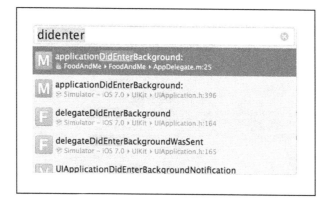

For a more refined search, you may want to select the search navigator from the navigator panel or use the keyboard shortcut *command + 3*. Typing a search query and pressing *enter* will prompt Xcode 5 to perform a project-wide search by default. The results will be displayed in the navigator below the search bar, and also includes new options for refinement. Selecting the **In Project** button (here, Project is the name of your project) will allow you to specify individual folders to perform the search in. For even more flexibility, the new search navigator will allow you to build custom search scopes that can be saved for future usage. The following screenshot shows the difference between when we do and when we do not select the **In FoodAndMe** button (in this case, FoodAndMe is the project name):

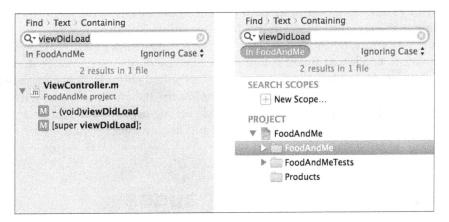

Top-level documentation

Apple provides some of the most in-depth SDK documentation of any development platform. Access to this documentation is possibly one of the most important aspects of iOS development. Previous versions of Xcode always had access to documentation; however, Xcode 5 takes a more accessible approach with its top-level documentation. It's important to note that an Internet connection is required unless you predownload the documentation from Apple. This can be done by navigating to **Xcode | Preferences | Downloads**.

Go to the menu bar and navigate to **Help | Documentation and API Reference**. Xcode 5 will show a separate window that has been designed to streamline the search and display of all of the documentation. Apple has built this documentation to work for you. As you type, Xcode will display suggestions in the form of API references, SDK guides, and even **Sample Code** related to your search.

The new documentation view also provides support for tabs, allowing you to view multiple pieces of documentation simultaneously. As you browse through the results, you may see a dynamic table of contents by clicking on the table of contents button immediately to the left-hand side of the search bar. The table of contents will automatically update based on the document you are currently viewing.

Additionally, the new documentation has built-in bookmarking, which allows you to save your most frequently viewed resources. To the right of the search bar, you will see a share button. Clicking on this button will show a menu with options to share or bookmark the current reference.

You may have also noticed a small bookmark icon on the left-hand side of each title or heading while scrolling through the documentation. You can even save specific sections of any API reference rather than saving the entire document. All of your bookmarks can be viewed in the navigator by clicking on the navigator button immediately on the left-hand side of the table of contents button. This view will also allow you to browse the entire documentation library at a glance. Combine this with the previous ability of pressing the *alt* key and clicking on any code to display an inline summary and linking from the code to full documentation, and then you'll have robust documentation integration!

Debugger and debug gauges

Debugging with Xcode 5 has been greatly improved thanks to many new features added to the debugger. Apple has completely switched from the previous GDB engine to the much more powerful LLDB engine. This allows breakpoint flexibility, inline variable previews, and the finding of variable values more easily.

If you have ever debugged a project using breakpoints, you will notice some changes in the way Xcode 5 manages its breakpoints. Breakpoints are still created by clicking directly on the required line number. These breakpoints can then be enabled or disabled by clicking on them directly or using the breakpoints button that has been moved to the debug toolbar found at the bottom of the Xcode window.

Each breakpoint may also be configured to respond conditionally. By default, code will stop once it reaches a breakpoint. Once you set conditions, however, breakpoints will be ignored unless these conditions are met. You can edit these conditions by right-clicking on an individual breakpoint and selecting **Edit Breakpoint**. From here, set your conditions and resultant actions. These actions can include logging a message to the console, running an AppleScript or Shell Script, and even playing a sound.

Another great feature of Xcode 5's debugger is the ability to preview variables and objects during debugging using data tips. While debugging your application, hover your mouse over a variable and its value will automatically appear below your cursor. This works for standard data types, such as strings, numeric types, and Boolean types.

Data tips are very powerful when it comes to objects as well. For instance, while in debug mode, hover your mouse over an image, and a summary of information will appear about this object. Selecting the eye-shaped icon will allow you to preview the actual image right in code, as shown in the following screenshot:

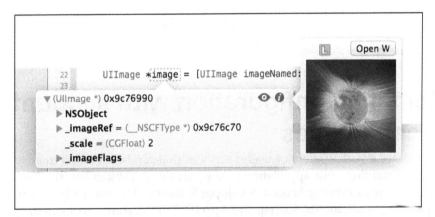

Properly debugging any application also involves monitoring system resources to ensure your code is as optimized as possible. Xcode 5 introduces **debug gauges**, a lightweight and embedded version of some useful instruments' tools. Because debug gauges are integrated into Xcode 5, they are able to run alongside the application at all times while allowing you to observe CPU, Memory, iCloud, Energy, and OpenGL ES resources.

Debug gauges can be found through the debug navigator and will begin running automatically once you run a project. The previously mentioned resources are displayed in an easy-to-read visual graph so that you can monitor your application's performance at a glance and in real time. Additionally, access to the complete instruments software is just a single click away, which is achieved by clicking on the **Profile in Instruments** button shown in the following screenshot:

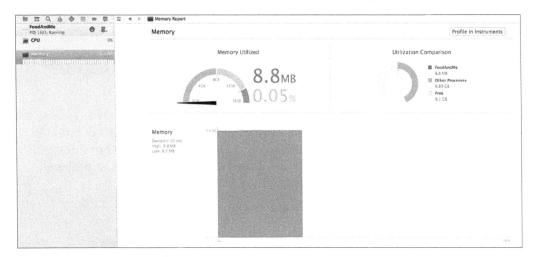

Automatic configuration with accounts and capabilities

Apple provides a wide variety of useful services that can be included in any application. Enabling your application to support these services has always been a hassle due to the number of tasks a developer is required to manually set up. These include adding entitlements, such as the App ID, linking frameworks to the project, and adding required fields to the projects .plist file. Additionally, each of these services has its own requirements, which means that supporting multiple services would require different steps to complete.

With the introduction of Xcode 5, Apple has made these struggles a thing of the past using automatic configuration. With automatic configuration, all a developer needs is an Apple ID linked to a developer account.

Navigate to **Xcode | Preferences** and select the **Accounts** section (new in Xcode 5). From here, you can add all your Developer Program Apple IDs and view details related to each account. Clicking on the **+** button located on the left-hand side panel will give you the option to add a new Apple ID. Doing so will provide a direct connection between Xcode 5 and the Apple Developer Portal. Once logged in, click on the **View Details...** button at the bottom-right corner of the screen. A new window will appear with details of all code-signing identities and provisioning profiles attached to the selected account.

Under the **General** tab in the project editor, you will see a new option, **Team**, found in the **Identity** section. Selecting this option will show you a list of identities related to the account we previously added. By selecting your respective signing identity, Xcode 5 will be able to verify whether you have all proper provision profiles and even offer to create them for you if required.

Potentially, the biggest advancement provided by automatic configuration is the **Capabilities** tab (new in Xcode 5) found in the project editor. This streamlined approach will allow you to configure specific platform features, such as **iCloud**, **In-App Purchases**, and **Game Center**, without having to visit the developer portal as shown in the following screenshot. Xcode 5 will automatically configure the provisioning profile, add App ID entitlements, and link all required frameworks for you, automatically:

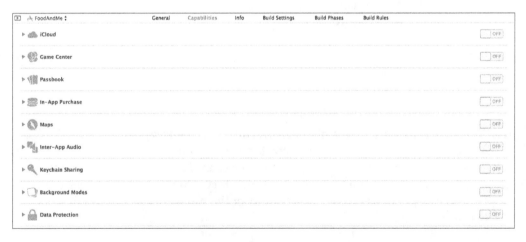

If you prefer to set up your features and capabilities the old way, you may still do so in the Apple Developer Portal.

Source control

Source control is widely used by large teams and individual developers alike. It provides an extremely useful way to track changes to code and revert back to stable builds of a project with version control. Teams of developers may work separately on individual components by creating and managing a copy of the code (called a **branch**) without overwriting another team member's code. The change will later be merged while simultaneously tracking all the changes made to the code base.

Source control is not a new feature of Xcode 5; however, Apple has decided to provide easier access to its functionality by creating a top-level menu item. Selecting it will display a drop-down menu with one-click access to most of the source control commands, such as commit, push, and pull. Hovering over **Working Copies** will open a new submenu that allows you to switch between branches, create a new branch, or merge branches. The following screenshot shows this submenu:

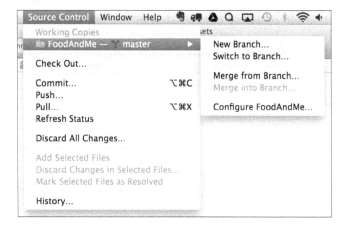

In addition to local source control on your computer, Xcode 5 also supports the ability to connect directly to remote repositories hosted on popular sites, such as GitHub. Open preferences and navigate to the **Accounts** tab once again. This time, after clicking on the **+** button, select **Add Repository**. Once you have entered the proper repository address, Xcode 5 will connect the repository, thus allowing you to access it remotely.

Asset catalogs

Every project you create will contain at least a few image files in the form of launch images and application icons as well as other UI elements. Asset catalogs serve two major purposes in Xcode 5. These include automation of icon and launch image naming conventions and grouping image files together in a single location.

Asset catalogs are represented as a separate group with a blue folder in the project navigator. By default, each new project created will include the default `Images.xcassets` item. You may also create your own asset catalogs for further organization based on personal preference.

Xcode 5 requires each of the launch image files and icon image files to be named appropriately based on the device and/or resolution the image will be used for. When selecting the `Images.xcassets` item, you will see a number of empty slots waiting for images to be added. Each slot has a description of what image it holds. Dragging from your computer into Xcode 5 on the respective slot will add the image to your project and automatically configure all the naming conventions. The following screenshot shows the **Asset Catalog** window:

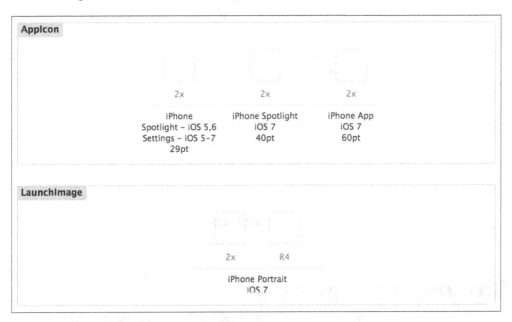

If you wish to add any additional images related to your project, you can simply drag-and-drop them into the **Asset Catalog** window, and Xcode 5 will take care of the rest. Both high-resolution (*2x*) and standard-resolution (*1x*) image files will be grouped together in their own image set with a common name. You still must provide both the low-resolution and high-resolution images yourself. Xcode 5 does not automatically scale them for you: it simply groups them. The value for this name can be changed to any value and will be used in code to access the associated images regardless of the actual filename.

Quick build device selection

Developing applications for multiple devices requires consistent device-specific testing. The iOS simulator included in the iOS SDK provides simulation for all Apple devices. With Xcode 5, selecting the proper device to build for has also been streamlined into a single drop-down option found on the toolbar.

Clicking on the name of the current device on the left of the toolbar will provide a drop-down menu. Any and all physical devices connected to your computer will appear on the top of the list (you may have to scroll up to see them), and all standard iOS simulator devices will appear below.

Simply select the device you wish to test for, and click on **Run**. The simulator will launch and switch to the selected device. The following screenshot lists the devices in the drop-down menu:

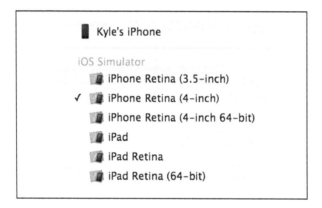

Storyboard previews

Up until now, writing applications that supported previous versions of iOS mostly consisted of updating API calls and minor coding conventions. With iOS 7, Apple has drastically changed the design of all standard UI objects. Knowing the size, position, and layout of all objects for both iOS 7 and previous versions is very important to maintaining a consistent user experience. This is where storyboard previews come in.

In order to use storyboard previews, you must select the assistant editor and navigate to the view you wish to preview (usually a .xib or .storyboard file). Select the **Related Files** menu option, navigate to **Preview**, and select the .xib or .storyboard file you wish to preview, as shown in the following screenshot:

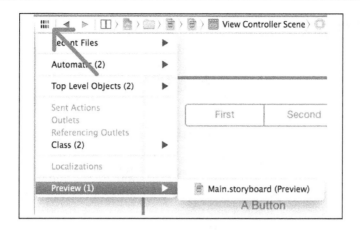

You will see an identical preview of your view on the right-hand side of the assistant editor. In the bottom-right corner of the view, you will see a button that says **iOS 7.0 and Later**. Click on it, and then select **iOS 6.1 and Earlier** as shown in the following screenshot:

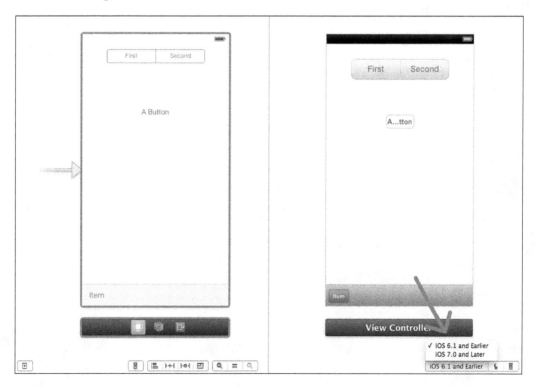

Your view will now display all of its UI elements as they will appear in iOS 6 or earlier. This is a very handy tool if you wish to make your app backwards compatible.

Summary

Xcode 5 has more features for developers than ever before, and each tool is designed to give you a more efficient experience while building the best quality apps possible. In this chapter, we learned how to use all of these features, from new debugging tools to automatic configuration. Although we covered a large portion of new Xcode 5 features, you should visit the following link to view Apple's documentation on what's new in Xcode 5: `https://developer.apple.com/library/mac/releasenotes/DeveloperTools/RN-Xcode/Introduction/Introduction.html`

With each new iOS SDK release, Apple includes some minor and some major updates to the Objective-C programming language. In the next chapter, we will cover the changes made to the Foundation Framework, possibly the most important framework in all of iOS development!

2
Foundation Framework – Growing Up

In this chapter, we will learn about modules and how they change the way we import frameworks into our files. We will cover both, the new and the old classes of the Foundation Framework, starting with the brand new `NSProgress` class. We will see some of the major improvements to the existing classes including `NSArray` and the `firstObject` method, `NSTimer`'s new property for managing tolerance, the additional encodings now supported by `NSData`, and lastly new ways to manage URLs with `NSURLUtilities`. Let's get started!

Why Foundation matters

Foundation is the core framework of Objective-C. Without it, developing iOS applications would not be possible. Foundation defines the base layer of all classes, as well as functionality for basic data types, including strings, arrays, and dictionaries.

Changes made to the Foundation Framework can range from minor enhancements to the introduction of completely new classes. iOS 7 is no exception to this and Apple has provided some great new features that we will explore in this chapter.

Modules

While developing applications using Xcode and the iOS SDK, you may have noticed that it has never been a requirement to import commonly used header files, such as `UIViewController.h` or `UIView.h`.

Open any file in any project, and navigate to any view-controller based .h file in the project. The very first line of code will read as follows:

```
#import <UIKit/UIKit.h>
```

Downloading the example code

You can download the example code files for all Packt books you have purchased from your account at http://www.packtpub.com. If you purchased this book elsewhere, you can visit http://www.packtpub.com/support and register to have the files e-mailed directly to you.

As an iOS developer, you have probably written hundreds of #import statements in any one project. When the compiler reaches an import statement, it literally inserts every line of code found in the imported header file. In the previous example of the first line of code, UIKit.h imports all header files available in the UIKit Framework; so, you don't have to worry about which header file should be imported for different instances.

If you have ever taken a look at all of the files included in UIKit, you will see that they total over 11,000 lines of code. This means that each file importing UIKit.h will grow by 11,000 lines of code. This is less than ideal; however, Apple provides one solution with **precompiled header (PCH)** files.

Precompiled headers – a partial solution

Each project you create will automatically generate its own PCH file in the supporting files group. During the preprocessing phase of compilation, the PCH file will load and cache the specified headers to import. The following is an example of a PCH file:

```
#import <Availability.h>

#ifndef __IPHONE_5_0
#warning "This project uses features only available
  in iOS SDK 5.0 and later."
#endif

#ifdef __OBJC__

  #import <UIKit/UIKit.h>
  #import <Foundation/Foundation.h>
  #import "UIImage+ImageEffects.h"

#endif
```

Your application may require a specific framework or class in multiple files. Rather than importing the file individually (and repeatedly), adding the import statement to the PCH file will precompute and cache a majority of the work during the preprocessing phase of compilation. This allows each file to be pulled from the cache when available.

Although this method works well, when importing the Apple frameworks, you must always remember to link the frameworks to your project. Failing to do so will result in a number of errors thrown by the compiler.

Modules – smart importing

With the introduction of iOS 7, Apple has introduced a new way to handle precompiling frameworks with modules. Instead of replacing an import statement with every line of code, a module encapsulates a framework into a self-contained block. Modules are precompiled in the same way import statements are precompiled in the PCH file; however, using modules will automatically link the proper framework and provide the exact same speed boost to compilation.

Modules are enabled by default in all new projects created using Xcode 5. For older projects, you can enable modules in your project's build settings by searching for modules and setting **Enable Modules (C and Objective-C)** to **Yes**.

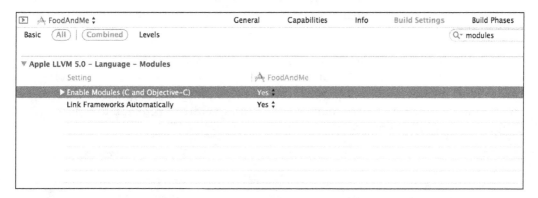

Now that modules have been turned on, you can start using the new syntax to import frameworks. At the top of the `.h` file you wish to import, simply type the following code:

```
@import QuartzCore;
```

That's all that is required in your code. Xcode will automatically link the required framework (in this case, `QuartzCore`) and provide you with all of the speed boosts for compilation.

Additionally, you can import specific header files based on need. You may, for instance, only require the `CoreAnimation` headers provided by `QuartzCore`. You can easily import these headers by typing the following:

```
@import QuartzCore.CoreAnimation;
```

Additionally, Xcode will automatically convert `#import` statements to `@import` for you at runtime. Although convenient, it is still recommended you update to new syntax whenever possible.

It is also important to note that modules currently only support Apple frameworks. Custom classes and third-party frameworks still require the traditional method or the PCH file.

NSProgress

iOS 7 introduces a completely new class to the Foundation framework, `NSProgress`. Using `NSProgress` involves treating each task of an action as a milestone of completion. By doing so, you, the developer, can track progress directly in code and perform individual tasks for each milestone.

For instance, to perform a particular action, you may require four separate tasks to be completed. Each task is capable of monitoring its own progress, and will report once the task is complete. In our example, this would increase the percent of completion to 25.

`NSProgress` uses **Key Value Observing (KVO)** to provide notifications related to progress. These notifications can be used to update a UI component displaying progress to the user, such as a progress bar or label. The following code is a very simple implementation that demonstrates working with `NSProgress` to report progress in a localized manner:

```objc
NSArray *data = @[@"Data 1", @"Data 2", @"Data 3", @"Data 4"];

self.dataProgress = [NSProgress
    progressWithTotalUnitCount:data.count];

int index = 0;

for (NSString *string in data) {

// Do something with string or other data
```

```
    index ++;
    self.dataProgress.completedUnitCount = index;


    NSLog(@"%@", [self.dataProgress localizedDescription]);


}
```

NSArray

When using NSArray, you must ensure that all supplied indexes are within range and not beyond the length of the array. When retrieving an element using an index, the index must be between zero and a number (the number being the total items in the array); otherwise, an exception will be thrown. A common use case of this involves grabbing the first or last object from an array.

NSArray has always had the following method to obtain the last object:

```
- (id)lastObject;
```

Previously, grabbing the first object of an array required checks to ensure that the index was within the bounds of the array, as shown in the following code snippet:

```
- (id)firstObjectInArray:(NSArray *)array {

  if (array.count > 0) {
    return array[0];
  }


}
```

Although the preceding example is rather small, you can see how more complex implementations can be complicated and time consuming. Thankfully, with iOS 7, Apple has finally made public a previously private method for NSArray to grab the first object:

```
- (id)firstObject;
```

This handy method will allow you to quickly access the first object of any array without the hassle. Additionally, if the array is empty, this method will return nil.

NSTimer

It is a common practice to perform periodic tasks using NSTimer. The following is an example use of NSTimer to perform a task in two-second intervals and repeats:

```
[NSTimer scheduledTimerWithTimeInterval:2.0
  target:self
  selector:@selector(targetMethod:)
  userInfo:nil
  repeats:YES];
```

The issue with this method is that the CPU is consistently active in order to perform the desired task repeatedly. When using multiple timers at once, it is possible (although unlikely) that it may reduce the performance of the CPU for the rest of your application. It is always best practice to run tests on your applications to find such possibilities and use safeguards wherever possible.

Apple has added a new tolerance property to NSTimer to reduce the strain on the CPU when using NSTimers. This property will tell the application how late a timer is allowed to fire when it has surpassed its scheduled interval. As a result, the application will be able to group actions together to reduce CPU strain.

This new property can be accessed and set with the following methods:

- (NSTimeInterval)tolerance;
- (void)setTolerance:(NSTimeInterval)tolerance;

Setting this property will help create safeguards for your CPU usage related to timers.

NSData

Every application uses data in some way or another. In some instances, you may require the ability to manipulate individual bytes of data. NSData encapsulates these raw bytes to allow for easy manipulation using built-in methods.

With iOS 7, NSData now adds support for Base64 encoding and decoding; a group of ACSII format binary-to-text encoding schemes. These schemes are most commonly used to transfer data between media that only support text-based data transfer. Encoding images from JSON-based responses from a web API is the most common use for these schemes.

Prior to iOS 7, developers were required to use a third-party library or build their own from scratch. Apple has made it exceptionally easy to use these encoding methods with the following methods:

- `(id)initWithBase64EncodedData:(NSData *)base64Data options:(NSDataBase64DecodingOptions)options;`

- `(NSData *)base64EncodedDataWithOptions: (NSDataBase64EncodingOptions)options;`

- `(id)initWithBase64EncodedString:(NSString *)base64String options:(NSDataBase64DecodingOptions)options;`

- `(NSString *)base64EncodedStringWithOptions: (NSDataBase64EncodingOptions)options;`

The first two methods are focused on UTF-8 encoded data, while the remaining two deal directly with string values. Both pairs of methods provide the same functionality; however, each use case may provide better performance.

NSURLUtilities

The Foundation Framework includes many different methods related to handling URLs; however, most API's related to manipulating these URLs are based on NSString because NSURL is an immutable class.

In order to fix this issue, Apple has introduced NSURLComponents to allow for manipulation of URL objects. With NSURLComponents, NSURL can be treated as a mutable object that allows direct manipulation. The following code snippet is an example use case:

```
NSURLComponents *components = [NSURLComponents
  componentsWithString:@"http://somewebsite.com"];

components.path = @"/somepath";
components.query = @"queryParameter=parameterValue";

NSLog(@"%@", [components URL]);
```

Running this code will output the following to the console:

`http://somewebsite.com/somepath?queryParameter=parameterValue`

Using NSURLComponents, you may now directly manipulate NSURL values without the use of NSString.

Summary

In this chapter, we covered some of the major updates to the Foundation Framework. It is always recommended that you stay up to date with the advancements to Objective-C and Apple's core frameworks. With this knowledge, you now have the tools to build more efficient and better-performing applications!

Now that we have a better understanding of the new features found in Foundation, it's time to start building our application. In the next chapter, we will begin building our interface using the new Auto Layout features in iOS 7.

3
Auto Layout 2.0

In this chapter, we will create our project and start building our application, **Food and Me**, starting with the custom menu view. First, we will create the project itself in Xcode 5. Next, we will create our storyboard. This consists of adding all the required elements and using the new Auto Layout to add constraints to our views. This is where we will dive directly into how Auto Layout works and how you will continue using Auto Layout for your future projects. Lastly, we will hook everything up to our code and set up our navigation. On completing this chapter, we will have a functional menu view complete with a bare navigation controller.

Why you should use Auto Layout

Prior to Auto Layout, building applications to dynamically support multiple screen sizes and orientations required large amounts of work. Auto-resizing masks, springs, and struts are all examples of the tools that developers would commonly struggle to use. These tools did not always produce the correct result, so the typical next best action was to detect screen sizes in code and adjust the layout accordingly. When working on an application with many views and layouts, this can become frustrating.

With iOS 6, Apple introduced a new feature called Auto Layout. The premise was pretty straightforward: allow developers to define constraints on all visual elements in a storyboard in order to control the layout and flow of an application. Unfortunately, Auto Layout caused many headaches.

The main issue was related to the fact that Auto Layout required every object to have proper constraints attached to it. If you failed to provide a single constraint, Xcode would generate it automatically, sometimes overriding some of your currently set constraints. This would commonly cause many layout issues at runtime, resulting in a poor user experience.

With iOS 7, Apple has completely revamped Auto Layout, making it much easier to provide layout constraints with simple tools and giving developers more control over each constraint.

Properly using Auto Layout will drastically reduce the time spent on building dynamic layouts. This is accomplished by replacing complex and cumbersome code with easily defined constraints created in our storyboard. Auto Layout does not provide a solution for everything, so it is important to decide when to use code versus when to use Auto Layout.

You can download all of the assets, including the completed project, by visiting the project's downloadable content and downloading the files to your computer. Let's get started!

Creating our project

We are going to use Auto Layout to set up constraints for our main menu of the **Food and Me** app. We will not be using Auto Layout for the entire application for the sake of simplicity, but we will be covering all of the necessary elements to learn how to use the new Auto Layout.

First, let's create a new project. Open Xcode and select **Create a new Xcode project** on the welcome screen (or navigate to **File** | **New** | **Project** from the menu bar if the welcome screen does not appear). Select **Single View Application** and then click on **Next**.

Fill in the template options as follows:

- **Product Name**: Food and Me
- **Organization Name**: Enter the name of your organization or company
- **Company Identifier**: Input your desired identifier that will be used on the developer portal, using reverse domain notation
- **Class Prefix**: Leave this option empty
- **Devices**: **iPhone**

Xcode creates a standard project for us, including the app delegate, a single view controller, a storyboard file, and an asset catalog for our launch image and icon. First, let's rename `ViewController.h` and `ViewController.m` to something more descriptive. Select `ViewController.h` in the navigator to show this file in the editor. Right-click on the `ViewController` text found immediately after `@interface`, and then navigate to **Refactor** | **Rename...**. It is possible for this refactor to sometimes skip renaming filenames in storyboards, so it is always a good practice to double-check this. Using snapshots and/or source control is another great way to reduce risk.

We will be creating the menu view in this file, so let's rename it `MenuViewController`. Type this in and make sure **Rename related files** is checked, and then click on **Preview**. A new window will appear giving you a preview of what files will be changed and where. You should see a header file and an implementation file in the preview as well as the storyboard (Xcode is smart enough to update every related project file). After clicking on the **Save** button, a prompt will appear asking if you would like to enable snapshots. This is similar to the **Source Control** menu and is completely optional.

Lastly, we need to add our image files to the provided Asset Catalog. Open the `Food and Me` folder that we downloaded earlier. You will see another folder titled `Final Image Files`. If you open this folder, you will see all the image files (both regular size and 2x retina size) used for our project. Switch to your Xcode project and select `Images.xcassets`. Drag-and-drop every single image in the `Final Images Files` folder onto the box that contains the `AppIcon` and `LaunchImage` set. A new image set will be created for each 2x and regular size image pair.

Starting our storyboard

Now that all of our files and images are added, we can start building our storyboard and apply Auto Layout constraints. Open `Main.storyboard` and we should see an empty view controller assigned to our `MenuViewController` class.

Our menu will be made up of four separate components. Let's start by adding the first three to our storyboard file (the fourth will be created programmatically). Open the Xcode **Utilities** pane (if it is not already open) and select the object library at the bottom of the view.

First, drag one `UIImageView` class onto our `MenuViewController` making sure it is sized to fit the entire view. Next, drag two `UIButton`s on top of the `UIImageView` without worrying about their position. In our **Utilities** pane, select the **Attributes Inspector**, and then select one of the two buttons. Erase the **Default Title** option so that it is blank. Next, click on the drop-down menu for **Image** and select `foodButton` as our image. Xcode will automatically resize `UIButton` to the dimensions of our button image. Repeat this process for the remaining `UIButton`, except this time select `addButton` for the image property in the **Attributes Inspector**.

Now reposition the buttons at the bottom of the screen, evenly spaced apart from one another. The exact position is not important, so adjust the position based on personal preference. The final view of the storyboard should now look similar to the following screenshot:

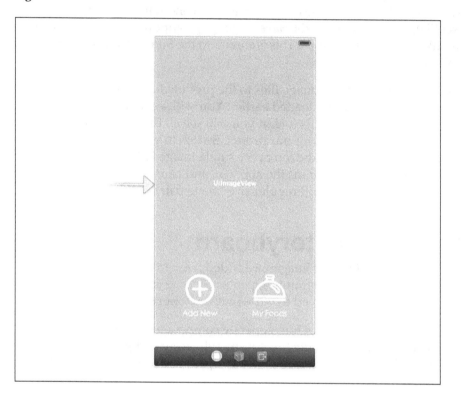

Setting up button actions

Our final step before applying our Auto Layout constraints is to connect our buttons to the class, using an IBAction for each button. While MenuViewController is selected, open the assistant editor from the toolbar and make sure you select the header file (MenuViewController.h).

While holding down the *control* key on your keyboard, click on and drag the **My Foods** button into the header file. Position your mouse between @interface and @end and release the mouse once you see a small popup that says **Inset Outlet, Action, or Outlet Collection**. In the new view that pops up, select **Action** from the **Connection** drop-down menu, and name this action myFoodsPressed. Lastly, select the **Type** drop-down option, and select UIButton. Repeat this process for **Add New** with an action name addNewPressed.

Your header file should now look like the following code snippet:

```
#import <UIKit/UIKit.h>

@interface MenuViewController : UIViewController

- (IBAction)myFoodsPressed:(UIButton *)sender;
- (IBAction)addNewPressed:(UIButton *)sender;


@end
```

Now that our view is populated and all actions have been created, we can get started with Auto Layout.

Using Auto Layout

Simply put, Auto Layout is a set of instructions given to each view related to the size and position in its superview or the nearest neighboring views. Two very common uses for Auto Layout is to make sure your views know what to do when an application runs on a 3.5-inch screen versus a 4-inch screen versus an iPad screen or when the device changes orientation. We want our application to support both screen sizes, so we will be focusing on this when adding our constraints.

Xcode provides multiple ways to apply your constraints, and each constraint also has its own properties that can be individually manipulated. With all of these options, I prefer to set up my Xcode environment to fully embrace all Auto Layout options.

Be sure that your **Utilities** pane is open. This will allow you to manually change your constraints' properties while working on your layouts. In the bottom-left corner of the storyboard view, you will see a button with an arrow pointing towards the right. This button will open the document outline view. This pane allows you to have a bird's-eye view of all view controllers and their subviews, including all constraints applied to each view. Open this view and your Xcode view should now look similar to the following screenshot:

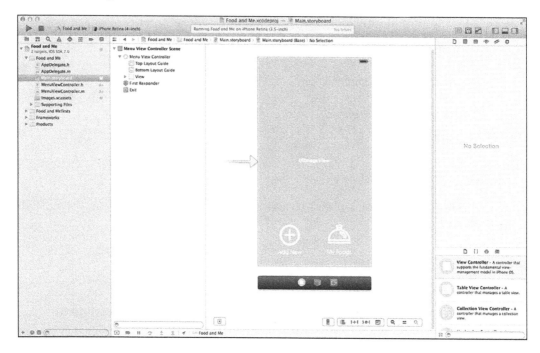

Applying constraints

Our menu view features two buttons to navigate to separate areas of the application. We want the buttons to always be in alignment with one another, so let's add some constraints to our buttons to make that happen.

One way to add a constraint between two objects is the control drag from one object to the other. Hold down the *control* key on your keyboard and then click-and-drag from the **Add New** button to the **My Foods** button. A new pop up will show these multiple options to add constraints. Each of these items can be selected and will provide the respective constraints between the two objects. Holding down the *shift* key will allow you to select more than one option at a time.

From the menu, select **Horizontal Spacing**. You will notice an orange outline appear around the **Add New** button, and a horizontal I-shaped line will appear between the two buttons, as shown in the following screenshot:

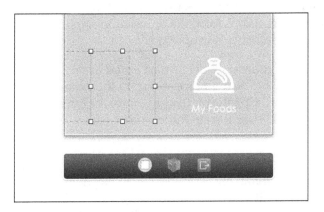

In order for Auto Layout to properly calculate the position of our views, it must have a complete set of constraints. All constraints will be highlighted in orange until a complete set of constraints is provided. Currently, we have only one constraint between the two buttons, which tells Xcode that these two views need to always remain an equal distance apart.

Let's add some more constraints. Each button should also remain vertically aligned, so let's add that constraint. This time, however, hold down the *command* key and select both buttons. With both items selected, Xcode 5 knows that any constraints provided will be applied to these two views. On the bottom-right corner of the storyboard view, you will notice a group of buttons as shown in the following screenshot:

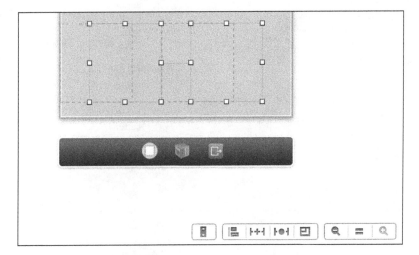

These buttons provide quick access to all Auto Layout options. With both buttons still selected, click on the second button in the group of four buttons as shown in the previous screenshot. A new pop up will appear (see the following image) with a complete list of options and properties to set/edit. You may have recognize some of these properties and constraints from the previous menu displayed when we used control dragging from one button to another.

We want to focus on alignment, which can be found at the bottom of the pop-up view. Check the box next to **Alignment**, and from the drop-down menu select **Top Edges**. Now click on **Add Constraint** to apply it to our button views. A new line will appear above both the buttons to indicate that both will always be top aligned to one another.

Our constraints will still appear orange, which means we still need to add more constraints for Xcode to make proper calculations. Xcode has detected this as well and provides a really great tool that provides suggestions based on what is required. In the document outline view to the left, a small red circle with an arrow has appeared next to **Menu View Controller Scene**. Clicking on this arrow will push a new view that lists all of the missing constraints and warnings.

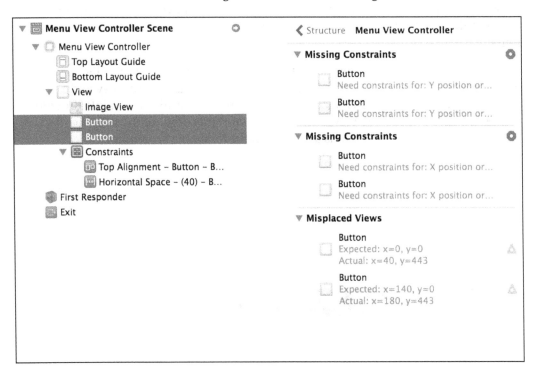

Our warnings are pointing to two very specific issues related to the X position and the Y position. We need to add constraints that will tell Xcode how to lay out the buttons' X and Y positions, so let's do that now.

Select just the **Add New** button. Our application has a pretty simple layout, and it is safe to say that we would prefer our buttons to keep an equal distance from the bottom of the screen regardless of size, so let's add a constraint that does just that. While keeping the button selected, navigate your mouse to the **Editor** menu option at the top of the screen, and select **Pin | Leading Space To Superview**. A new I-shaped bar appears between the edge of the view and the **Add New** button. This will make sure that an equal distance is kept between the button and the main view.

Now that we have taken care of the X position, let's do the same for the Y position. Select **Editor | Pin | Bottom Space To Superview**. A new bar appears from the bottom of the button to the bottom of the screen. This will make sure there is an equal distance between the button and the bottom of the screen.

With this new constraint, all of our constraints have now turned blue, which means Xcode has all the information it needs to calculate the positions of our views! You may be wondering how this is the case, when we have not added these superview constraints to the **My Foods** button.

The answer is that we don't need to. The first couple of constraints we added actually take care of this for us. Both buttons will always stay top aligned, which will take care of the Y position of the other button. Additionally, we set the horizontal spacing between the buttons, which will automatically take care of the other button's X position. The following image illustrates how this is possible:

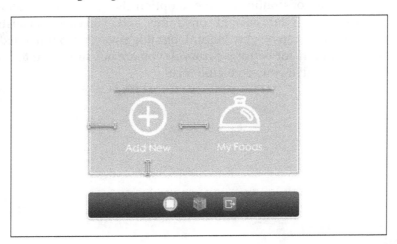

Now that our constraints are set up, let's set the background image. Select the image view we added earlier, and in the **Attributes Inspector**, set the image to Background. Now go ahead and run the application first on the 4-inch iPhone and then on the 3.5-inch iPhone. The buttons at the bottom of our screen will automatically position themselves based on our constraints, and we didn't have to write a single line of code to do so!

Resolving Auto Layout issues

After seeing our application running on an iPhone, it may be in our best interest to move the buttons down just a bit for a more balanced layout. Return to Xcode, and select both buttons by holding down the *command* key and clicking on each. Move them down a few pixels based on preference.

You will notice that suddenly there are two dashed red lines surrounding our buttons. Xcode does not automatically update constraints when a view is manually repositioned, so now the previous calculations are no longer valid. The dashed red lines let you know there is an error with our constraints that requires correction.

Thankfully, Xcode has some handy features available to help correct these issues. From the menu bar, navigate to **Editor** | **Resolve Auto Layout Issues** | **Update Constraints**. This can also be accomplished using the fourth button to the bottom-right corner of the storyboard. By selecting this, Xcode will recalculate the previous constraints based on our view's current physical position. The whole of the error will now disappear with no issues.

In addition to updating constraints, this menu option also gives you the ability to add missing constraints, update current constraints, and even clear all constraints. These automated options can be very helpful, but it is always recommended to set your constraints manually for better accuracy. If you are not sure what to do next, these options may also give you some guidance.

Finishing our menu view

Our buttons tend to blend into the background slightly, so let's add a new view that will help them stand out better. First, let's navigate to our storyboard and create a new outlet for our background image. Select our `MenuViewController` class, and open the assistant editor. Control drag from the background image in our storyboard to the `MenuViewController.h` file (between `@interface` and `@end`). Name this outlet `mainBackground`. Now switch to `MenuViewController.m`, and add the following code to `ViewDidLoad`:

```
// Create a white transparent bar for the bottom of the screen
// Set the color to white with an alpha of 0.5
UIView *bottomBarBG = [
  [UIView alloc] initWithFrame:CGRectMake(0,
  self.view.bounds.size.height - 130,
  self.view.bounds.size.width, 130)];
bottomBarBG.backgroundColor = [
  UIColor colorWithWhite:1.0f alpha:0.5f];

// Add the view to the background
    [self.view insertSubview:bottomBarBG
      aboveSubview:self.mainBackground];
```

The first line creates a new `UIView` and sets its frame. We set its Y position based on the screen height to guarantee that regardless of screen size, the `UIview` will be at the very bottom of the view.

Next, we set the background color to be solid white and set the alpha to `0.5` (half) so that the view appears slightly transparent.

Lastly, we add the button background view to our main view. We know that our button background should be above the main background but below the buttons, so we insert the view using `aboveSubview` so that it will always be directly above the main background. Run the application and take a look at the final design of our menu.

Preparing for navigation

The last thing we need to do is add a navigation controller for our view. This will be required to display (or push) our **My Foods** view. We can accomplish this in our storyboards with a single click of a menu item.

Switch to our `Main.storyboard` and then select `MenuViewController`. From the top menu bar, navigate to **Editor** | **Embed In** | **Navigation Controller**. Xcode will automatically add a navigation controller to the storyboard, set our `MenuViewController` as the root view controller, and then set our new navigation controller as the initial view to load. Our storyboard will now look like the following screenshot:

We don't want our menu view to display the navigation bar, so let's switch back to `MenuViewController.m` and add the following final line of code to `viewDidLoad`:

```
[self.navigationController setNavigationBarHidden:YES];
```

Summary

In this chapter, we covered the new features of Auto Layout by building our menu view and applying constraints. Now that you have a good understanding of the new features of Auto Layout and how to use them, I highly recommend that you practice all the different types of constraints available on multiple views. Auto Layout is very powerful and, when used correctly, will eliminate a large portion of code normally attributed to dynamic layouts!

In the next chapter, we will continue by building the next part of our application. We will explore some of the new design principles of iOS 7 and apply them to our app, **Food and Me**.

4
Building Our Application for iOS 7

We'll start the chapter by covering some of the new design principles present in iOS 7. This includes changes to the navigation and status bars, to the new UIKit, and changes to the application icon. Next, we will create our required files and organize them for easier navigation. Lastly, we will add some new view controllers to our storyboard and point them to our newly created files. On completing this chapter, we will have a complete skeleton of our application that is ready for functionality. Let's get started!

Designing for iOS 7

With the release of iOS 7, developers and designers will need to adjust their approach to suit the new "flat" design. Although it is not a requirement to follow this design pattern, almost all UI elements in the SDK have been completely revamped to support it.

It is important to consider these changes when designing your iOS 7 application in order to keep a balanced layout. Some factors include new typography and updated UIKit dimensions. In this chapter, we will put together the skeleton of our application, but first we will discuss two important changes to iOS 7 that will directly affect how you build your future applications.

The navigation bar and status bar

Probably, the most apparent change to iOS 7 is the new navigation bar and status bar. Both of these items have been around since the launch of iOS. Prior to iOS 7, the 20-pixel status bar was simply a solid background view that would cover the top 20 pixels of the main application window.

Additionally, when using a navigation controller, the navigation bar itself would also act in the same manner, covering the next 44 pixels (for a total of 64 pixels) of the view. Because of this, an item positioned with a $y=0$ value would be positioned directly below the navigation or status bar.

With the release of iOS 7, this has been removed entirely. The status bar itself now contains a clear background allowing any UI elements or views to be positioned behind it. Run our application and notice how our menu background image extends to the top of the device's screen, directly behind the status bar as shown in the following screenshot:

It is very common for most applications to have the status bar background match the navigation bar background. In iOS 7, setting the navigation bar color will automatically set the status bar background to match. The following screenshot is an example from our completed application:

Another result of this change is that programmatically positioning your views on the y axis requires you to consider the heights of the status bar and the navigation bar. A view positioned at $x=0$ and $y=0$ will appear on the top-left corner of the screen, behind the navigation and status bar.

It is important to understand that this change specifically applies to code that is executed at runtime. When using storyboards, this new positioning does not apply. Xcode will automatically adjust views in storyboards in relation to the navigation and status bars. Each view will retain its initial y position regardless of any adjustments made.

Lastly, Apple has added a new translucent property to the navigation bar. Open the contacts application on any device running iOS 7 and scroll through your contacts. You will notice that as each item passes behind the navigation bar, it can be seen through the bar as it moves off the screen. This effect is used throughout iOS 7 and its newly designed applications, and Apple has also made it available to be used by developers. By default, this property will be set to YES, but can be disabled at any time if you wish.

The new UIKit

iOS 7's new flat design has changed many of the dimensions of common UIKit elements. Some of these include segmented controls, search display controllers, and alert views. Most of these changes result in a smaller frame than found on previous versions of iOS, but also include updated typography and user interaction. The newly designed search bar is as shown in the following screenshot:

The segmented controls are as shown in the following screenshot:

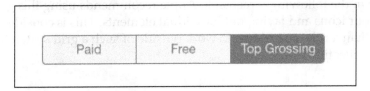

The new alert view for a notification is as shown in the following screenshot:

The new alert view for deletion is as shown in the following screenshot:

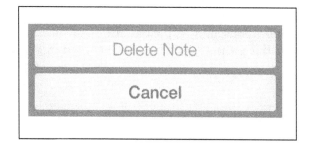

Updated app icons

Apple has made a subtle change to the standard iOS application icon size with the release of iOS 7. Previously, icons featured an even corner radius that was easy to replicate on your own. Apple has provided a new shape known as a **superellipse** with a more stretched corner radius. Additionally, the shine (gloss effect) has been removed from application icons. As always, Xcode 5 will automatically clip your app icon images to the proper shape; however, if you wish to add your own stroke or shadows, you will need to use an unofficial template.

Additionally, Apple has introduced what they call a **golden ratio grid system** that you will see in the following screenshot. Apple recommends using this grid when designing your icons and laying out individual elements. This is considered more of a guideline than a rule, so feel free to work outside of such a grid system if it better suits your application icon.

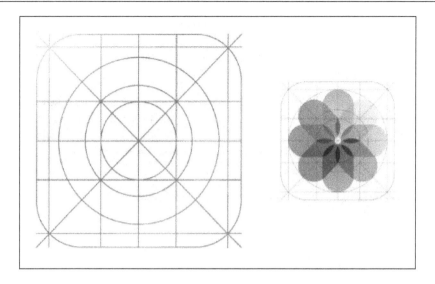

Putting together the pieces

Now that we have covered some of the basic design aspects of iOS 7, it's time to start building our application skeleton. Before we write any code, let's create the essential project files, construct our views in our storyboard, and create/connect outlets for each view controller. We will be able to navigate through our application; however, it just won't do anything yet.

Project organization

One of the first steps in my development process is organizing my project in Xcode 5. Doing so makes it easier to navigate your project and find the files you need. Let's go ahead and organize our app.

Open our **Food and Me** project and take a look at the navigator on the left. We have a couple of files in no particular order, and we will also be creating more files shortly. We are going to divide our main project files into the following three separate categories:

- App Delegate
- View Controllers
- Custom Classes

On the navigator pane, right-click on the top-level folder (Food and Me, our application name) and click on **New Group**. A new group will appear in our main Food and Me group; let's name it App Delegate. Repeat this process two more times, naming the new groups View Controllers and Custom Classes, respectively.

Select both AppDelegate.h and AppDelegate.m (using the *command* key) and drag these files into the App Delegate group we just created. Do the same for MenuViewController.h and MenuViewController.m and drag these files into the View Controllers group. These groups can also be rearranged, so feel free to move them around based on preference.

The following screenshot gives a peek into the final results found in the Food and Me project:

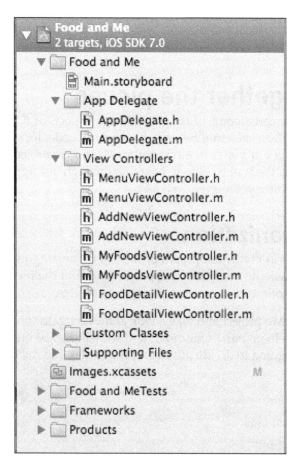

Creating the files

Now that our project is a little more organized, it's time to create our remaining project files. Our application will require a view controller for our menu, the addition of new foods, views of our current foods, and then a detailed view of each food item. We have already set up our menu, so let's create the remaining files.

Right-click on our `View Controllers` group and click on **New File** (you can also achieve this by navigating to **File | New | File** in the menu bar). Make sure that **Cocoa Touch** is selected in the left-hand side menu bar, select **Objective-C class** from the options, and then click on **Next**. Name this file `AddNewViewController` and make sure it is a subclass of `UIViewController`. Click on **Next** and then on **Create**. Our new file will be created and added to our `View Controllers` group.

Repeat this process two more times. The first file will be named `MyFoodsViewController` and will be a subclass of `UITableViewController`. Name the second file `FoodDetailViewController` and set it as a subclass of `UIViewController`. We now have most of our required files for our application. In a later chapter, we will be creating one last project file in our `Custom Classes` group.

Setting up the storyboard

Now that we have our files, we need to create some views in our storyboard and hook them up to our classes we just created. Open `Main.storyboard` and you should see our navigation controller and its root view controller (the menu view controller). Let's add the remaining controllers to our storyboard now.

Open the **Utilities** pane on the right-hand side (if not already open) and click on the **Object Library**. Our `AddNewViewController` and `FoodDetailViewController` files are both subclasses of `UIViewController`, so drag two view controller objects onto the storyboard. Our `MyFoodsViewController` is a subclass of `UITableViewController`, so let's drag a `UITableViewController` object onto the storyboard as well.

Select one of the `UIViewControllers` and open the identity inspector. In the custom class section at the top, set this `View Controllers` class to `AddNewViewController`. Now select the remaining `UIViewController` and set its class to `FoodDetailViewController`. Lastly, select our `UITableViewController` and set its class to `MyFoodsViewController`. Our storyboard now has all of the objects needed for our application.

AddNewViewController

Now that we have created our files and added the proper controllers to our storyboard, let's go ahead and add the required objects to each controller. We will start with the `AddNewViewController` object. Select it, and then navigate to **Object Library** in the **Utilities** pane.

Our application will give users the ability to track what they eat. Each food item will consist of an image, name/title, and the date it was created. We will need to provide an image view to store the final image, a placeholder image view, and a `UITextField` object to input the name of the food item.

Drag a `UITextField` object and two `UIImageView` objects onto the `AddNewViewController` view. These will allow our user to interact with the view and create food items for our app. In this chapter, we are simply adding all the elements to our project, so do not worry about the size or positions of these objects.

Select the `AddNewViewController` object itself and then click on the assistant editor button (the middle button in the top-right corner that resembles a tuxedo). Switch to `AddNewViewController.h` if it is not already displayed. In order to access these objects in our code, we will create outlets for each item in our code. While holding down the *control* key on your keyboard, click-and-drag from the `UITextField` to the header file and let go. Name this outlet `nameTextField` and click on **Connect**. Repeat this for both `UIImageViews`. Name the first image view `placeholderImageView` and the second `finalImageView`. We now have all required objects and connections for `AddNewViewController`.

FoodDetailViewController

When a user selects one of their previously added food items, we want to display a detailed view that includes a fullscreen background image, an image of the food, the name of the food, and then finally the date it was saved. Select the `FoodDetailViewController` class in the storyboard, and navigate back to the **Utilities** pane and the **Object Library**.

Drag two `UIImageViews` and two `UILabels` onto the food detail view. Once again, ignore the size and positioning of each item. We will also add outlets for each object to our code, so go ahead and open the assistant editor and switch to the `FoodDetailViewController.h` file. Control drag from the first image view to the space between `@interface` and `@end` in the `.h` file, and name the outlet `backgroundImageView`. Perform the same steps for the second image view and name it `foodImageView`.

Our labels will be used to display the name and date related to the food item. Control drag from the first label and name this outlet `foodNameLabel`. The second `UILabel` should be named `foodDateLabel`. We now have all the views required for our `FoodDetailViewController` class.

MyFoodsViewController

When we dragged the `UITableViewController` object to the storyboard, Xcode 5 automatically added a `UITableView` object, with a plane prototype cell, to the controller. **Food and Me** will be using a custom `UITableViewCell` subclass to create and lay out our table view cells. This will be covered in a later chapter, so for the time being we will make one simple change to the `MyFoodsViewController` class. Select the prototype cell and a small white box will appear at the bottom of the cell's frame. Click-and-drag down this box to resize the cell. Set its height to 100 pixels, as shown in the following screenshot:

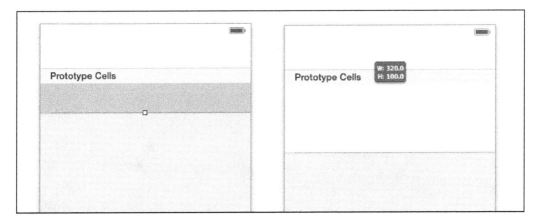

Summary

In this chapter, we learned some of the newer design principles associated with iOS 7. Additionally, we organized our project, created all of our required files, and started our views in storyboard. We are ready to start writing some code and adding functionality to our application.

In the next chapter, we will finish building the `AddNewViewController` class and add the functionality to save our users' data for later viewing.

5
Creating and Saving User Data

In this chapter, we will start by adjusting the style of our navigation bar to match the navigation style of iOS 7. Next, we will create our buttons in the navigation bar and hook them up to the proper methods. Once we adjust our storyboard, we can start writing the code to allow a user to take or pick an image, give the item a title, and then back up the data to disk for later use. On completing this chapter, our application will have all the functionality required for users to save new food items!

Picking up where we left off

In the last chapter, we created all our files and then connected them to our storyboard. We then added all of the required elements (labels, image views, and so on) to each view controller. Last, we created outlets and connected them to our storyboard elements. The purpose of this chapter, along with that of the following chapter, is to finish building the application. We will be implementing one portion of the core functionality, which is the ability to take or select a photo, add a name, and then save the data. Once we complete this, we can start using some of the new features of iOS 7 to add additional visual appeal to our application.

The navigation bar style

Before we move on, let's go ahead and alter some of the navigation bar style options. Our application will have the same navigation bar style in every view, so our best approach is to use the appearance proxy on `UINavigationBar` in our `AppDelegate` object. This will allow us to write the code only once, and the navigation bars in the entire application will abide by these styles.

Switch to `AppDelegate.m` and scroll down to the `applicationDidFinishLaunchingWithOptions` method. We are going to set the color of the navigation bar, the font for the title label, and the navigation bar tint color (this will change the color of the bar button items on the navigation bar). Additionally, our application will have text-based bar button items, so we want to set the appearance proxy on `UIBarButtonItem` to match our application style. Copy and paste the following code into `applicationDidFinishLaunchingWithOptions`:

```
[[UINavigationBar appearance] setBarTintColor:
  [UIColor colorWithRed:200.0//255 green:0.0/255 blue:
  23.0/255 alpha:1.0f]];
[[UINavigationBar appearance] setTitleTextAttributes:
  @{NSForegroundColorAttributeName: [UIColor whiteColor],

  NSFontAttributeName:
  [UIFont fontWithName:@"HelveticaNeue" size:19.0f] }];

[[UINavigationBar appearance] setTintColor:[UIColor whiteColor]];

[[UIBarButtonItem appearance] setTitleTextAttributes:
  @{NSFontAttributeName:[UIFont fontWithName:
  @"HelveticaNeue-Light" size:18.0f]} forState:
  UIControlStateNormal];
```

First, we set the color of the navigation bar base to dark red. Next, we set the title text font color to white and set its font to a specific font. You can replace this font with any font you wish; I just like the way this font looks. To match our title text, all navigation bar buttons should also be white, so we set the `navigationTintColor` method (do not get confused with the `navigationBarTintColor` method, which will change the color of the navigation bar itself and not the navigation items) to white. Last, we alter the font of our `UIBarButtonItem` objects to match our navigation bar title style.

Now that our navigation bar is styled, let's add some code to our
`MenuViewController` to finalize the style of our application. Switch to
`MenuViewController.m` and scroll down to the `viewDidLoad` method. First,
let's adjust the background color of the menu buttons. Previously, we set the
`backgroundColor` property to white, but let's change this to match our dark red
navigation bar. Replace the previous background color code with the following
code snippet:

```
bottomBarBG.backgroundColor = [UIColor colorWithRed:200.0/255
green:0.0/255 blue:23.0/255 alpha:0.7f];
```

Last, write the following code into the `viewDidLoad` method:

```
// Set this in every view controller so that the back button
   displays back instead of the root view controller name
self.navigationItem.backBarButtonItem = [[UIBarButtonItem alloc]
   initWithTitle:@" " style:UIBarButtonItemStylePlain target:nil
   action:nil];
```

This is a very handy piece of code to use. By default, when a `viewController`
method is pushed onto the navigation stack, it will display a back button (less-than
sign) and text. The text is based on the previous view controller's title. We want to
only display the < symbol, so we add the previous line of code. We are basically
telling the application that for every back button, the text should be equal to `@""`,
or an empty string. It is worth noting that this can be changed by setting the back
button property of the navigation item in our storyboard. The following screenshot is
an example of our application before and after introducing an empty string:

Adding our button action

Our next step is to add the code to be called when the **Add New** button is pressed. In our previous chapter, we created an action called `addNewPressed` and connected it to our **Add New** button. Let's go ahead and write the code to present the proper view controller when this button is pressed. First, switch to `MenuViewController.h`, and directly underneath the standard `#import` for UIKit, let's import our view controllers as shown in the following code snippet:

```
#import <UIKit/UIKit.h>
#import "AddNewViewController.h"
#import "MyFoodsViewController.h"

#define ADD_NEW_VIEW_CONTROLLER @"AddNew"
```

We have also defined a string literal for our storyboard ID for good practice. We have named it `ADD_NEW_VIEW_CONTROLLER` so that we know what it contains. Switch back to `MenuViewController.m` and scroll down to our `addNewPressed` method. As we will be presenting this view controller (dragging it onto the screen from the bottom), we need to also create a navigation controller to hold the `AddNewViewController` object. The following is the code for adding a button action:

```
- (IBAction)addNewPressed:(UIButton *)sender {

// Present the addNewFoodViewController
AddNewViewController *vc = [self.storyboard
  instantiateViewControllerWithIdentifier:
  ADD_NEW_VIEW_CONTROLLER ];"];
UINavigationController *nav =
  [[UINavigationController alloc] initWithRootViewController:vc];

[self.navigationController presentViewController:
  nav animated:YES completion:nil];

}
```

This code is pretty straightforward. We allocate our `AddNewViewController` object by initializing it from our storyboard. Make sure that `AddNewViewController` in our storyboard has the property for our storyboard ID set to `AddNew` so that it matches our string literal defined earlier. Under certain circumstances, it is recommended to preinitialize the view controller before presenting it if there is a noticeable lag between the button press and the view being presented. Next, we create a navigation controller and assign our newly created `AddNewViewController` as its root view controller. Last, we tell the current navigation controller to present the new one. Go ahead and run the application and test the functionality. The `AddNewViewController` object inside of a navigation controller should slide onto the screen.

Adding buttons to our navigation bar

You may have noticed that when presenting our `AddNewViewController` object, we have no way to dismiss the view to get back to the menu. Let's add this functionality now. We will be creating two bar button items that will be text-only items. The first button, **Cancel**, will dismiss the view while the second, **Save**, will save the new food entry.

Switch to `AddNewViewController.m` and scroll down to `viewDidLoad`. Add the following code at the top of `viewDidLoad`:

```
// Add our bar button items
    UIBarButtonItem *cancelButton = [[UIBarButtonItem alloc]
        initWithBarButtonSystemItem:UIBarButtonSystemItemCancel
        target:self action:@selector(cancelButtonPressed:)];
    UIBarButtonItem *saveButton = [[UIBarButtonItem alloc]
        initWithBarButtonSystemItem:UIBarButtonSystemItemSave
        target:self action:@selector(saveButtonPressed:)];

    // Assign the bar buttons to the navigation controller
    [self.navigationItem setLeftBarButtonItem:cancelButton];
    [self.navigationItem setRightBarButtonItem:saveButton];
```

Here, we create both bar button items using the built-in **Cancel** and **Save** bar button items provided by iOS. Each button also has its own selector (or method) that we will code in a moment. Next, we assign each bar button to the navigation bar. I chose to place **Cancel** on the left-hand side and **Save** on the right-hand side of the bar; however, this order is entirely up to you. If we run our application and click on the **Add New** button, our view will slide into place, and you will see **Cancel** on the left-hand side and **Save** on the right-hand side. Our appearance proxies defined in the app delegate should also be reflected in the font and text color. Next, let's actually add the **Cancel** button functionality.

Switch back to `AddNewViewController.m` and scroll down to the bottom of `viewDidLoad`. We want to allow the user to cancel adding a food item, so let's write the `cancelButtonPressed` method that we earlier assigned to our cancel button. Directly below `viewDidLoad`, add the following code:

```
- (void)cancelButtonPressed:(UIButton *)sender {

    // Dismiss the view
    [self.presentingViewController
      dismissViewControllerAnimated:YES completion:nil];

}

- (void)saveButtonPressed:(UIButton *)sender {


}
```

We have defined both our `cancelButtonPressed` and `saveButtonPressed` methods here (`saveButtonPressed` has been intentionally left blank until later in the chapter). In `cancelButtonPressed`, we simply tell the view controller to dismiss itself and set the animated view controller to YES. Run the application and test this functionality.

Adjusting our storyboard view

Now that we have some of our code implemented, we need to finish arranging our view in `Main.storyboard`. Previously, we only added the required elements and did not position or size them correctly. Switch to `Main.storyboard` and scroll down to the `AddNewViewController` object.

We have three items to position and size here, starting with the two image views. Select the first image view, and in the **Utilities** pane, select the **Size Inspector** submenu. Set the width and height to 180 pixels to create a perfect square. Position this image view horizontally in the center of the view and slightly higher than the vertical center of the view. Do not worry about being precise, and feel free to position the image view where you think it looks best!

Repeat this process for the other image view, making it an identical size and in exactly the same position. For this image view, switch to the **Attributes Inspector** submenu (in the **Utilities** pane on the right-hand side) and set its image to `placeholder_image` for `placeholderImageView`. Using the documents outline, make sure that this image view is positioned *below* the other image view. We will be using two image views to assist in save validation. When a user selects or takes an image, it will be set to the top image view (the empty one) and cover the placeholder image view beneath it. This allows us to check if the top image view contains an image. If it does not, it means the user has not added an image and that the placeholder is still visible. In this case, we will alert the user to let him/her know that he/she must include a photo.

Last, we need to adjust the settings of our `UITextField` object that will be used to type in the name of our food entry. Select the text field and reopen the **Size Inspector** submenu from the **Utilities** pane. Set the height to 38 pixels and the width to 280 pixels. Position the text field horizontally centered and slightly above the image views.

Select the **Attributes Inspector** from the **Utilities** pane and change the following settings:

- **Alignment**: Select the Center icon
- **Placeholder**: `Type The Food Name`
- **Border Style**: This field should be set to none (the first of the four buttons)
- **Capitalization**: Select Words

The final result should look something like the following screenshot:

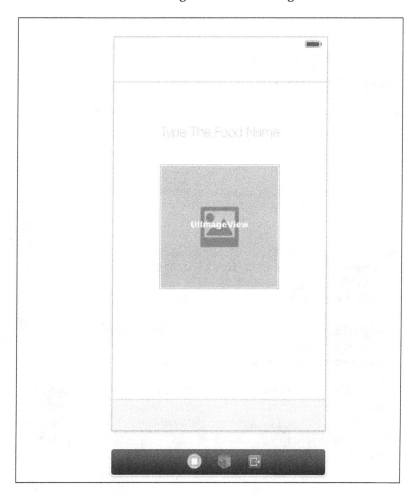

Adding our delegates

Now that our view is completely set up, we can start coding the desired functionality. Before we can move on, we need to specify some delegates that our view controller will require to work. We will work with a text field, image picker, navigation controller, and action sheet, all of which have their own custom delegates. Switch to `AddNewViewController.h` and replace the line of code after `#import` with the following code:

```
@interface AddNewViewController : UIViewController
  <UITextFieldDelegate, UIActionSheetDelegate,
  UIImagePickerControllerDelegate, UINavigationControllerDelegate>
```

Here, we are simply specifying the protocols that our class will conform to in the code. With this final step, we can now start coding our functionality into the application!

Using a tap gesture

For our application, a user can tap on the placeholder image in order to take or select a photo. To do this, we will add a tap gesture recognizer directly to the placeholder image view. Switch to `AddNewViewController.m` and scroll down to `viewDidLoad`. Add the following code at the bottom of the `viewDidLoad` file:

```
// Add a border around our image view
[self.placeholderImageView.layer setBorderWidth:6.0f];
[self.placeholderImageView.layer setBorderColor:[UIColor
  colorWithRed:129.0/255.0 green:129.0/255.0 blue:130.0/255.0
  alpha:1.0].CGColor];

UITapGestureRecognizer *imageViewTapGesture =
  [[UITapGestureRecognizer alloc] initWithTarget:self
  action:@selector(imageViewTapped:)];
[imageViewTapGesture setNumberOfTapsRequired:1];];

[self.placeholderImageView setUserInteractionEnabled:YES];
[self.placeholderImageView
  addGestureRecognizer:imageViewTapGesture];
```

First, we add a border and a corner radius to our image view for visual effect. Next, we create a tap gesture recognizer and assign it a method. We also set the property `numberOfTapsRequired` to `1`. The last step is to set the user interaction enabled on our placeholder image view to `YES` and then add our gesture recognizer to it. Now, our image view will keep listening for a single tap and call our `imageViewTapped` method when a tap is detected.

When the image is tapped, we want to give the user an option to either select an image from their library or take a new one using the camera. The best way to do this is using an action sheet. Let's create the `imageViewTapped` method, have it display an action sheet, and then respond to the users' selection accordingly. Below the `ButtonPressed` methods, add the following code:

```
#pragma mark - User Interaction Methods

- (void)imageViewTapped:(id)sender {

    [[[UIActionSheet alloc] initWithTitle:nil
                            delegate:self
                 cancelButtonTitle:@"Cancel"
              destructiveButtonTitle:nil
                    otherButtonTitles:@"Take Picture", @"Choose
                        From Library", nil]
        showInView:self.view];

}
```

With this code, when the user taps on the image view, we create an action sheet and display it in the current view. We only need the **Cancel** button and two additional buttons, one for **Take Picture** and another for **Choose From Library**. In order for us to respond accordingly to the selected action sheet button, we need to implement the action sheet delegate method. Below the `imageViewTapped` method, add the following code:

```
#pragma mark - Action Sheet Delegate

- (void)actionSheet:(UIActionSheet *)actionSheet
clickedButtonAtIndex:(NSInteger)buttonIndex {

    if (buttonIndex == actionSheet.cancelButtonIndex) {
        return;
    }

    if (buttonIndex == 0 && [UIImagePickerController
      isSourceTypeAvailable:
      UIImagePickerControllerSourceTypeCamera]) {
        // Take Picture Selected
        UIImagePickerController *imagePicker =
          [[UIImagePickerController alloc] init];
        imagePicker.delegate = self;
        imagePicker.allowsEditing = YES;
```

```
        [imagePicker setSourceType:
          UIImagePickerControllerSourceTypeCamera];

        [self.navigationController presentViewController:
          imagePicker animated:YES completion:nil];

    }


    if (buttonIndex == 1) {
        // Choose Photo From Library
        UIImagePickerController *imagePicker =
          [[UIImagePickerController alloc] init];
        imagePicker.delegate = self;
        imagePicker.allowsEditing = YES;
        [imagePicker setSourceType:
          UIImagePickerControllerSourceTypePhotoLibrary];

        [self.navigationController presentViewController:
          imagePicker animated:YES completion:nil];

    }

}
```

In this method, we first check if the selected button is the **Cancel** button, and if so, we return to end the execution of this method, which will also hide the action sheet for us. Next, we check if the button index is equal to 0, or `Take Picture`. If so, we create an instance of `UIImagePickerController`. We set the delegate to `self` and also allow editing (this will allow the user to crop the image into a perfect square, which is ideal for our application), and then we set the source type to camera.

If the button index is 1, or `Choose From Library`, we use exactly the same code with one exception. For this block, set the source type to photo library to display the phone's camera library. Save our code and run the application. Everything should work as expected.

Getting the image from UIImagePickerController

Now that a user can take a photo or select from their phone's photo library, we need to grab that image and display it. In order to do so, we need to implement the image picker's delegate method, the `didFinishPickingMediaWithInfo` method. Below our action sheet delegate method, add the following code:

```
#pragma mark - UIImagePicker Delegate

- (void)imagePickerController:(UIImagePickerController *)
  picker didFinishPickingMediaWithInfo:(NSDictionary *)info {

    UIImage *pic;

    //Grab the stored image
    if ([info objectForKey:UIImagePickerControllerEditedImage]) {
        pic = [info objectForKey:
          UIImagePickerControllerEditedImage];

    [self.finalImageView setImage:pic];
    [self.placeholderImageView setHidden:YES];

    }



    [self.presentingViewController dismissViewControllerAnimated:
      YES completion:nil];


}
```

In this method, we create an instance of `UIImage` and assign it using the info dictionary provided by the image picker. Because we want our users to edit the image, we want to grab the edited version instead of the original (which can be accessed using `UIImagePickerControllerOriginalImage`). Now that we have our final image, we assign it to our final image view and then hide the placeholder image view. Last, we need to tell the image picker controller to dismiss itself to bring us back to our `AddNewViewController`.

Save everything and run the code to test it out. If you wish to actually take a picture with the camera, you must run this on an actual device.

Adding the text field delegate

Now that we have our image, we need to set up the text field delegate. This is probably the simplest of all delegate methods because we only need to tell the application what to do when the *return* key is pressed. For our application, we simply want to hide the keyboard. Below our image picker delegate method, add the following code:

```
#pragma mark - Text Field Delegate

- (BOOL)textFieldShouldReturn:(UITextField *)textField {

    [textField resignFirstResponder];
    return NO;
}
```

This method simply tells the text view to resign first responder (hide the keyboard) when the *return* key is pressed. A user can type in a name, press the *return* key, and hide the keyboard. Make sure that the text fields delegate property has been set to AddNewViewController (self) either in the storyboard or in viewDidLoad.

Saving the data

We now have everything we need from the user to create a new food entry. In order to save the data, we will need to follow multiple steps so that we can access it again later in the app. The save data method we created earlier will be quite long once complete, so we will cover it piece by piece for simplicity, starting with a custom date helper method.

Getting the date string

For our application, we will be creating a .plist file that will store the food entry's name, date created, and the file path to the image. The image itself will be saved separately in the documents directory. When saving any file to the documents directory, you must specify a filename. In order to save multiple images, we need to make sure that every single image file saved has a different filename. One of the best (and most popular) ways to accomplish this is using a date.

Each device keeps track of the current date down to the millisecond. This means that at any given millisecond, the date will be completely different from every date before and every date after. This gives a great way to create a unique identifier for each image based on when it was created. What we will do is grab the current date, set the date format, and convert it to a string that we will then tack onto the end of each filename. This way, every single image will have a unique filename that will be stored in our `.plist` file to be accessed later.

I have created a simple helper method that returns the current date as a string value that we can use for the filename, so let's add it to our code. Scroll down to the end of the last method and add the following code:

```
#pragma mark - Date Helper Method

-(NSString*)stringForCurrentDateTime
{
    NSDateFormatter *format = [[NSDateFormatter alloc] init];
    [format setDateFormat:@"yyyyMMddHHmmss"];


    NSDate *now = [NSDate date];
    NSString *dateString = [format stringFromDate:now];

    return dateString;
}
```

With this code, we first create a date formatter that takes the year, month, day, hour, minute, and second values of a date and pushes them together. Next, we create a date object and set it to the current date and time. Finally, we create a string using our date formatter and return it. Now that we have our helper method, let's add the code to save the data!

Adding validation

We are now ready to implement the `saveButtonPressed` method. Before we write any of the code to actually save the date, we first need to check that the user has actually selected an image and added a name. This will prevent us from having any errors and will guarantee that we have the required data. Scroll down to the empty `saveButtonPressed` method we created earlier and add the following code:

```
- (void)saveButtonPressed:(UIButton *)sender {

// Check if the image and title have been saved
// If so, save the image to the documents directory and dismiss
   the view

    if (self.finalImageView.image &&
      self.nameTextField.text.length > 0) {
        // Image and name have been set, so we can save




    } else {

        [[[UIAlertView alloc] initWithTitle:@"Missing Data"
                                   message:@"A title and image
                                      are both required to save."
                                   delegate:nil
                          cancelButtonTitle:@"Ok"
                          otherButtonTitles:nil]
        show];

    }

}
```

This validation is very simple but effective. Here, we put to use having multiple image views by checking whether the final image view is nil. We also check to make sure that a user has actually added text to the text field by checking that the text property's length is greater than zero. If either of these two conditions is false, we display an alert view telling the user that both a title and an image are required to be saved. If both are true, we can proceed with our saving process. It is recommended that you use a data model to maintain data in an application; however, for our application, this will do fine.

Saving the image

The first step in the saving process is to save the image itself to the documents directory. Inside the first `if` statement block, add the following code:

```
// get paths from root direcory and the main documents directory
    NSArray *paths = NSSearchPathForDirectoriesInDomains
      (NSDocumentDirectory, NSUserDomainMask, YES);
    NSString *documentsPath = [paths firstObject];


// Set up and save our image to the documents directory
    NSString *imagePath = [documentsPath
      stringByAppendingPathComponent:[NSString
      stringWithFormat:@"image-%@", [self
      stringFromCurrentDateTime]]];

    NSData* data = UIImagePNGRepresentation
      (self.finalImageView.image);
    [data writeToFile:imagePath atomically:YES];
```

First, we grab the first element (which will always be the path to the documents directory) from the list of directories in the file system. We then create a new path for our image by adding a filename to the end of the documents path. The filename is how we access the image later in our app. Using our date helper method, we set the filename to image, and the returned date string is separated by a hyphen. Now every image will be found in the documents directly with a unique filename. Last, we create an instance of `NSData`, assign the user's final image to it as data using `UIImagePNGRepresentation`, and then save the date to the image path created previously.

Now that our image has been saved, we can save the rest of our data.

Creating versus loading the .plist file

In order to save the users' data, we will be creating a dictionary that contains all relevant data for each food entry. We will then add this dictionary to a `.plist` file and save the `.plist` file to the documents directory. To make sure we don't save over our previous data, we must first check to see if our `.plist` file already exists. Below the previous code for saving the image, add the following code:

```
    // Get the path to our Data/plist file and where we will be saving our
    images
    NSString *plistPath = [documentsPath
      stringByAppendingPathComponent:@"Data.plist"];

    // Forward reference of our array
    NSMutableArray *plistDataArray;

    // Call the file manager to check if the file exists
    NSFileManager *defaultManager = [NSFileManager defaultManager];
    if ([defaultManager fileExistsAtPath:plistPath])
    {
        // Assign the data
        // Get the current data from the plist file if it exists
        plistDataArray = [NSMutableArray
          arrayWithContentsOfFile:plistPath];

    }
    else
    {
        //create empty file
        NSMutableArray *array = [NSMutableArray array];
        [array writeToFile:plistPath atomically:YES];
        plistDataArray = [NSMutableArray
          arrayWithContentsOfFile:plistPath];

    }
```

First, we create another path by adding Data.plist to the end of the documents directory created earlier (this name can be anything you wish as long as it ends in .plist). Next, we create an empty array to hold the final .plist data and allow us to append more data to the end of the file. We create an instance of NSFileManager and use it to check if the file at the newly created path exists. If so, we set the contents of our .plist file to the plistDataArray method.

If the .plist file does not exist, we instead create another empty array, save the array as a .plist file, and then set the plistDataArray method to the content of the newly created (but empty) .plist file. Now we can add more data.

Adding a new entry

Now, we will grab the user data and turn it into a dictionary so that we can add it to our data array. Then, we can save it to the documents directory. Add the following code after the previous code:

```
// Create a new food item
NSMutableDictionary *foodItem = [[NSMutableDictionary alloc]
    init];
[foodItem setValue:self.nameTextField.text forKey:@"name"];
[foodItem setValue:imagePath forKey:@"image_filepath"];
[foodItem setValue:[NSDate date] forKey:@"date"];


[plistDataArray addObject:foodItem];
[plistDataArray writeToFile:plistPath atomically:YES];


[self dismissViewControllerAnimated:YES completion:nil];
```

Here, we create a new empty mutable dictionary. The dictionary is then filled with the user-entered name, the image path used earlier, and the current date and time. We then add this dictionary to our `plistDataArray` method and tell it to save (write) the file. Last, we dismiss the view controller to bring us back to the menu where we started, and our data has been saved!

Summary

In this chapter, we built the most important component of our application, the ability to create new food entries. Now that all of this data has been saved, we can retrieve it and start displaying it to our user. Because everything is saved directly to the device, we are able to manipulate this data instantly and use it as we please.

In the next chapter, we will build the final piece of our application's core functionality: viewing the user-created data both in a table view and in a detail view.

6
Displaying User Data

We have almost completed our application; however, we still have one last major piece of functionality to add. Now that our users can add content, they need to be able to view that data. In this chapter, we will put together a custom cell, build a table view to display a list of data, and build a detail view of the items when a user selects an item from the list. On completing this chapter, we will have a fully functional application.

We will begin by putting together our custom cell in the storyboard. Next, we will add a button to the navigation bar so that users can add food while viewing their current food items. Then, we will set up the table view, load our data, and pass the data to the table view. Lastly, we will implement the detail view of the items when a user selects an item from the table view. Let's get started!

Custom cell

Before we start writing our code to display the data, we want to create a custom table view cell. With your project open, select **File** | **New** | **File**. Select **Cocoa Touch** as the base and select **Objective-C Class** before clicking on **Next**. We want this class to be a subclass of `UITableViewCell`. The cell will display food items, so let's give it the name `FoodCell`. Save this file and move it into our **Custom Class** group (if it is not already in it).

Now that we have our class, let's link it up to our storyboard. Open `Main.storyboard` and find the table view controller we had previously moved into the storyboard. After opening the `Main.storyboard` file, open the **Utilities** pane and select the **Identity** section. Make sure that this view controller's class has been set to `MyFoodsViewController`. Now select the blank table view cell and set its class to our newly created `FoodCell` class.

Building the cell

Now that our class is linked, we can build the cell in our storyboard. The cell itself will consist of a `UIImageView` object and two `UILabel` instances. Open the **Utilities** pane and perform the following steps:

1. Drag a `UIImageView` object onto the cell itself to add it.
2. Set both the width and height to 100 pixels.
3. Position the image view to the far left of the cell.
4. Drag two `UILabel` instances onto the cell, positioned one above the other.
5. From the **Attributes** pane, set the font family of the top label to **Helvetica Neue**.
6. Set the style to **Ultra Light**.
7. Set the size to `20`.
8. Repeat this for the second (bottom) cell, but set the size to `11`.
9. Set both labels to be left aligned.
10. Position the labels horizontally to your preference.

Once completed, your cell should look similar to the following screenshot:

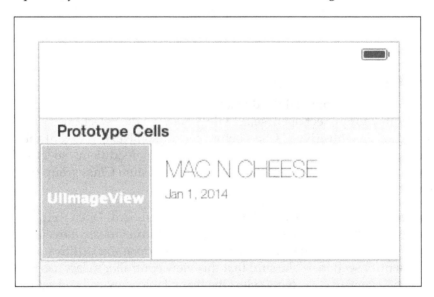

Connecting the cell

Now that our cell is visually laid out, we need to connect it to the class we created earlier; perform the following steps to connect this cell to our class:

1. Select the entire cell and then select the assistance editor. Make sure that we are viewing `FoodCell.h` in the right panel.

2. Control drag from the image to create an outlet named `foodImageView`. We want to avoid naming it just `imageView` because this property already exists by default on `UITableViewCell`.

3. Do the same for both labels giving them the names `foodNameLabel` and `dateAddedLabel`, respectively.

Creating properties

Now that our cell is ready, let's start coding `MyFoodsViewController`. This class will be loading the saved user data in order to display it, so we need to create an array property to hold the data. Additionally, we want our dates to be displayed in a user-friendly format, so let's also create a date formatter property. The date formatter is a useful class provided by Apple that allows you to manipulate the format of dates based on specific patterns. This is helpful considering that different locales require different formatted dates. Switch to `MyFoodsViewController.h` and add the following code:

```
#import <UIKit/UIKit.h>
#import "FoodCell.h"
#import "AddNewViewController.h"
#import "FoodDetailViewController.h"

@interface MyFoodsViewController : UITableViewController

@property (strong, nonatomic) NSArray *myFoodsArray;
@property (strong, nonatomic) NSDateFormatter *dateFormatter;

@end
```

In the preceding code, we simply created both the required properties. In addition to viewing the food items already created, a user will have the ability to create new items from this view too. In order to support this, we import the custom cell we created as well as the `AddNewViewController` class. We also imported the `FoodDetailViewController` class so that we can display our detail view.

Adding food

The first thing we want to do is give the user the ability to add additional food items from this view. The best way to do this is to add a button in the navigation bar. Apple provides a system button to add items that will be displayed as a nice plus button. Switch to `MyFoodsViewController.m` and scroll down to the `viewDidLoad` method. Add the following code:

```
// Set our views title
self.title = @"MY FOODS";

// Create the plus button
UIBarButtonItem *plusButton = [[UIBarButtonItem alloc]
    initWithBarButtonSystemItem:UIBarButtonSystemItemAdd target:self
    action:@selector(addButtonPressed:)];

    // Assign the bar buttons to the navigation controller
[self.navigationItem setRightBarButtonItem:plusButton];

// Set this in every view controller so that the back button
    displays the back button only without the viewcontroller name
self.navigationItem.backBarButtonItem = [[UIBarButtonItem alloc]
    initWithTitle:@" " style:UIBarButtonItemStylePlain target:nil
    action:nil];
```

Here, we create a new `UIBarButtonItem` property to go on the navigation bar. We have set the button to system item add to give us that plus button. Next, we tell the navigation controller to add this button as a right-hand side bar button item so it will show up on the right-hand side of the navigation bar.

Additionally, we set the title of the navigation controller and adjust the back button text. By default, iOS will add the previous view controller's title to the back button. For our application design, we simply want the back button icon only with no text. This line of code can be added to any view controller you wish to replicate this functionality.

Lastly, we want to implement the same `addButtonPressed` method we used in our `MenuViewController`. Add this code below `viewDidLoad`:

```
- (void)addButtonPressed:(id)sender {

    // Present the addNewFoodViewController
    AddNewViewController *vc = [self.storyboard
        instantiateViewControllerWithIdentifier:@"AddNew"];
    UINavigationController *nav = [[UINavigationController alloc]
        initWithRootViewController:vc];

    [self.navigationController presentViewController:nav
        animated:YES completion:nil];

}
```

Preparing the table view

Before we load any data, let's go ahead and set up our table view. To do so, we will be editing our table view delegate methods that Xcode automatically created for us. Scroll down to the `numberOfSectionInTableview` method and change the return value from 0 to 1.

The next delegate method we should implement is `numberOfRowsInSection`. This number will frequently change, so instead of hard coding the number as in the previous method, we will set this to the count of `myFoodsArray`. Every time the array is updated, the table view will also be updated.

The next method to update is `cellForRowAtIndexPath`. The default code will work just fine as long as we update the class name and cell identifier. Replace `Cell` with `FoodCell` and change the class declaration from `UITableViewCell` to `FoodCell`.

Lastly, we need to add an additional delegate method that was not added. Below `cellForRowAtIndexPath`, type - `table`, and a list of possible methods will appear. Scroll through, find `didSelectRowAtIndexPath`, and select it. Xcode 5 will automatically type the remainder of the method call. Be sure to include the opening and closing brackets of the method.

Your code should look like the following code:

```objc
#pragma mark - Tableview Methods

- (NSInteger)numberOfSectionsInTableView:(UITableView *)tableView
{
    // Return the number of sections.
    return 1;
}

- (NSInteger)tableView:(UITableView *)tableView
  numberOfRowsInSection:(NSInteger)section
{
    // Return the number of rows in the section.
    return self.myFoodsArray.count;
}

- (UITableViewCell *)tableView:(UITableView *)tableView
  cellForRowAtIndexPath:(NSIndexPath *)indexPath
{
    NSString *CellIdentifier = @"FoodCell";
    FoodCell *cell = [tableView
      dequeueReusableCellWithIdentifier:CellIdentifier
      forIndexPath:indexPath];

    // Configure the cell...

    return cell;
}


- (void)tableView:(UITableView *)tableView
  didSelectRowAtIndexPath:(NSIndexPath *)indexPath {


}
```

Loading data

It's time to load our data so that we can display it in the table view. Loading the data is very similar to the way we checked for files and saved the data in the previous chapter, because both require a specified path in the documents directory to be defined. For our application, we will create a method to load the data and return an array.

Place the following code below the addButtonPressed method:

```
- (void)loadFoodFromDocumentsDirectory {

    // Get paths from root directory and the main documents
      directory
    NSArray *paths = NSSearchPathForDirectoriesInDomains
      (NSDocumentDirectory, NSUserDomainMask, YES);
    NSString *documentsPath = [paths objectAtIndex:0];

    // Get the path to our Data/plist file and where we will be
      saving our images
    NSString *plistPath = [documentsPath
      stringByAppendingPathComponent:@"Data.plist"];

    // Call the file manager to check if the file exists
    NSFileManager *defaultManager = [NSFileManager
      defaultManager];
    if ([defaultManager fileExistsAtPath:plistPath])
    {
        // Assign the data
        // Get the current data from the plist file if it exists
        self.myFoodsArray = [NSMutableArray
          arrayWithContentsOfFile:plistPath];
        [self.tableView reloadData];

    }
    else
    {
        // Do nothing
    }

}
```

This code should be somewhat familiar. First, we create an array of paths using `NSDocumentsDirectory` and assign the path to the documents directory to a string. Next, we define the path to the file we want to load, in this case the `Data.plist` file we created previously. We allocate an `NSFileManager` instance and use it to check if the specified file exists at that path. If so, we assign the contents of the file to `self.myFoodsArray` and then reload the table view. Now, we have loaded all data (if any) and passed that data on to the table view.

Displaying data

With our data loaded, we can now display the data in our custom cell. Scroll down to `cellForRowAtIndexPath` and let's set up our cell.

First, we need to grab the current food item from our array. We will do this using the `indexPath.row` parameter passed to `cellForRowAtIndexPath`. Add the following line of code below our cell allocation and before `return cell`:

```
// Create an instance of the current food item
NSDictionary *currentFoodItem = self.myFoodsArray[indexPath.row];
```

Now that we have `currentFoodItem`, we can start assigning our custom cells properties. Let's begin with the image. Add the following code to `cellForRowAtIndexPath`:

```
// Grab the image from the current food item and set the cell
   image
UIImage *foodImage = [UIImage
   imageWithContentsOfFile:currentFoodItem[@"image_filepath"]];
cell.foodImageView.image = foodImage;
```

Here, we simply allocate an image based on the `image_filepath` key we created for each food item. Next, we set this image as the current cell's image. Now, we can set the text for the name of the food item with the following code:

```
// Set the name of the food
cell.foodNameLabel.text = [currentFoodItem objectForKey:@"name"];
```

The last item to update in our cell is the date the food item was added. We need to actually create our date formatter before this will work; so, let's do that now. Allocating date formatters can be very CPU-intensive, so we are creating a property that is allocated only once, rather than each time a cell is loaded. Scroll down to the `viewDidLoad` method and add the following code:

```
// Set the date formatter
self.dateFormatter = [[NSDateFormatter alloc] init];
[self.dateFormatter setDateFormat:@"MMM d, YYYY"];
```

First, we allocate and initialize our `NSDateFormatter` property. Next, we set the date format. The format we have chosen will display the month as a word, the day number in the month, and the year with all the digits. With all of this in place, run your code to test it. If you don't have any food items yet, go ahead and add some from this view to test its functionality.

Lastly, add the following final code to `cellForRowAtIndexPath`:

```
// Set the date using our date formatter
cell.dateAddedLabel.text = [self.dateFormatter
  stringFromDate:[currentFoodItem[@"date"]];
```

Here, we set the date of the cell to the current items date in the format specified by our date formatter.

Showing the detail view

When selecting one of the food items, the user should be directed to a new view with the capacity to display more details. All of the code to do this will be handled in `didSelectRowAtIndexPath`.

Before we write the code to push our detail view, we are going to adjust its layout. Switch to `Main.storyboard`, locate the `FoodDetailViewController` object, and perform the following steps:

1. Select one of the image views and size it to fit the entire screen. This will be our background image, so it must be the back layer as well. If needed, use the document outline to arrange the views.

2. Select the remaining image view and set its size to 200 x 200 square pixels. Position it centered horizontally and towards the top of the screen. This will be the food items' large image.

3. Next, move the two labels in the view to just below the second image (the food image). Select the first label and open the **Attributes Inspector** from the **Utilities** pane. Set the font to **Helvetica Neue Thin** with a size of 24. Now, change to the **Size Inspector** and set the label's width to 280 and height to 32. Position this label centered horizontally and just below the food image.

4. Select the second label and set its font to **Helvetica Neue Thin** of size 13. Also, change its width to 280 and height to 26. Also, position this label centered horizontally just below the name label.

Everything in our storyboard is how we need it for the final app! The following screenshot is what your `FoodDetailViewController` should look like:

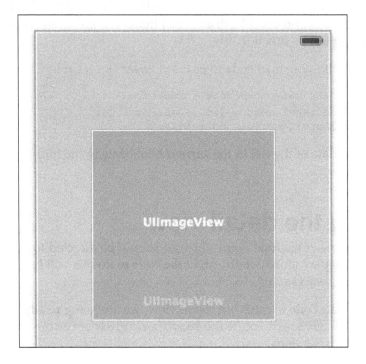

Coding the detail view

When pushing the detail view, we will pass the food item dictionary as a property so that we can display the data related to that food item in the detail view. To do this, let's add a property. Switch to `FoodDetailViewController.h`, and beneath our `IBOutlets`, add the following property:

```
@property (strong, nonatomic) NSDictionary *foodItem;
```

Creating blurred images

Now, we can pass a food item to this view controller. Next, we want to set the background image of the detail view. For our application, we are going to use our food image itself as the background image. Before we set the image, we will blur it and apply a dark tint to create a nice blurred image effect.

In order to do this, we will be using a `UIImage` category provided by Apple on the Apple Developer Portal. I have packed this category with the resources file available for download with this book. Open the provided `Food And Me` folder that was downloaded earlier from the Packt Publishing website (if you have not downloaded these files, you can find them by visiting this link in your browser: `http://www.packtpub.com/`) and then open the `Apple Code` folder. You will find a `.h` file and a `.m` file titled `UIImage+ImageEffects`. Drag these files to your project and make sure you check the copied items into the destination project folder.

Now that we have the files in our project, we need to import them. Add this import statement below `#import <UIKit/UIKit.h>`:

```
#import "UIImage+ImageEffects.h"
```

Let's put this category to use. Switch to `FoodDetailViewController.m`, and inside `viewDidLoad`, add the following code:

```
UIColor *tintColor = [UIColor colorWithWhite:0.11 alpha:0.36];

UIImage *foodImage = [UIImage imageWithContentsOfFile:[self.foodItem
objectForKey:@"image_filepath"]];

UIImage *blurredBackground = [foodImage applyBlurWithRadius:8
tintColor:tintColor saturationDeltaFactor:1.2 maskImage:nil];

self.backgroundImageView.image = blurredBackground;
```

First, we define a tint color for the image. We want it to be darkened so that white text is easily visible on bright food images. Next, we create a `UIImage` object using the `image_filepath` key from our `foodItem` property.

The next line is where the magic happens. We create a new `UIImage` instance and assign it using a method from the `ImageEffects` category. This method takes a few parameters.

The radius will determine how blurry the image will be. For best results, pick a value between **1** and **12**.

Tint Color is the color of the tint we would like on the image. You can set this to any color you wish based on each app's design.

`SaturationDeltaFactor` will adjust the saturation of the image. The lower the value of `SaturationDeltaFactor`, the more dull the image will be.

Masking the image allows you to pass in an image mask for more advanced blur shapes.

The last line of code sets the background image to the food image so that our background is completely filled; double-check the storyboard and make sure that the background image has been set to the mode **Aspect Fill**.

The following screenshot is a before-and-after example:

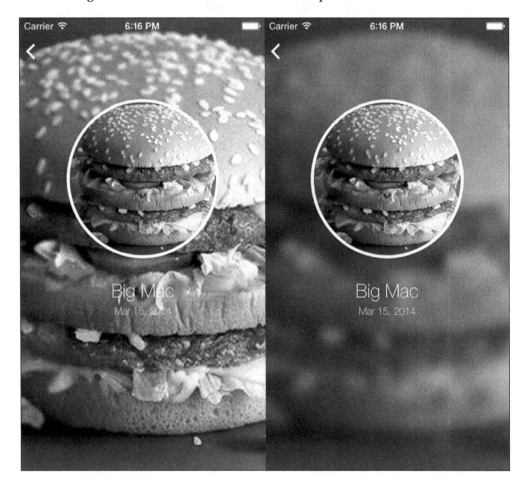

All of these parameters can be adjusted to your liking based on preference and/or app design.

Finishing our detail view

Now that we have our background image, let's fill in the rest of the information. First, we will start with our regular food image. Add the following code to `viewDidLoad`:

```
self.foodImageView.image = foodImage;

[self.foodImageView.layer
    setCornerRadius:self.foodImageView.frame.size.width / 2];
[self.foodImageView.layer setBorderWidth:4.0f];
[self.foodImageView.layer setBorderColor:[UIColor
    whiteColor].CGColor];
```

By reusing the `foodImage` object and setting it to the `foodImageView` property, we save a few lines of code. Here, we also add a corner radius to create a round circle image and apply a white border with a width of four pixels.

Now, we can write the code to display the name and date. Add the following code to `viewDidLoad`:

```
self.foodNameLabel.text = [self.foodItem objectForKey:@"name"];

    // Set the date formatter
NSDateFormatter *dateFormatter = [[NSDateFormatter alloc] init];
[dateFormatter setDateFormat:@"MMM d, YYYY"];

self.foodDateLabel.text = [dateFormatter
    stringFromDate:self.foodItem[@"date"]];
```

First, we set our name based on the `foodItem` property. Our date should be in the same format as in our table view cell, so we use identical code to create an `NSDateFormatter` object and set its format. Now, we use that date formatter to set our date text.

Pushing the detail view

Now that we have completed our detail view, we can start creating and pushing it onto the stack when a user selects their food items. Switch to `MyFoodViewController.m` and scroll down to `didSelectRowAtIndexPath`. Add the following code:

```
// Create an instance of the current food item
    NSDictionary *currentFoodItem = [self.myFoodsArray
      objectAtIndex:indexPath.row];

    FoodDetailViewController *vc = [self.storyboard
      instantiateViewControllerWithIdentifier:@"Food_Detail"];
    vc.foodItem = currentFoodItem;

    [self.navigationController pushViewController:vc
      animated:YES];
```

This code grabs the currently selected food item using `indexPath.row`. Next, we allocate an instance of our `FoodDetailViewController` we just created and set its `foodItem` property to the currently selected food item. Lastly, we push the `viewController` onto the navigation stack. Go ahead, run your application, and test out all functionality.

Summary

In this chapter, we finished our base application by adding the last piece of functionality, displaying the users' saved data in a table view and creating the detail view. We also learned how to create a blurred image using the `UIImage+ImageEffects` category provided by Apple.

Now that we have completed our application, we can learn how to use TextKit and manipulate text in iOS 7. We will then apply some of these new features to our application to spice it up a bit!

7
Manipulating Text with TextKit

We will start this chapter with an overview of the new UIKit hierarchy. From there, we will dive directly into the dynamic text type to support OS-wide font and size settings. Next, we will cover some of the new features, such as exclusion paths to wrap texts around shapes and adding a letterpress effect with a few lines of code. Last, we will discuss how to apply standard formatting to your text, such as underlined text. Let's get started!

What is TextKit?

Prior to iOS 6, providing mixed styles for your text was available using **UIWebView** and HTML markup or using the lower level framework **Core Text**. With the launch of iOS 6, Apple introduced attributed strings, allowing developers to adjust color and font attributes on defined subsections of any string. The first 10 characters could be set to a color of yellow and the remaining characters a bold font.

In iOS 6, text-based UIKit controls were based on both Core Graphics and WebKit. Here is a diagram to illustrate the hierarchy:

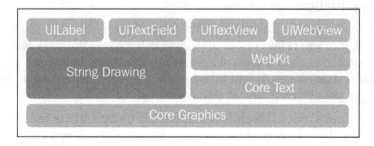

You will notice that **UITextView** actually uses **WebKit** itself for the sake of drawing attributed text using HTML. Although attributed strings provided many solutions for working with text, they were limited in flexibility for advanced layouts. This multi-line rendered text required the use of **Core Text**. This framework is very difficult to work with and understand.

With iOS 7, Apple has introduced **TextKit** to streamline working with text. Apple now inherits **UITextView** from **TextKit** rather than **WebKit** as illustrated in the following figure:

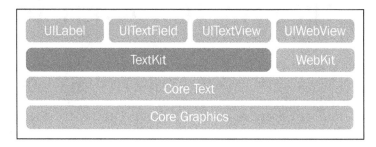

TextKit inherits all of the power found in **Core Text** (it is built on top of **Core Text**) and provides it in an easy-to-use and much improved API. All text-based UIKit controls (with the exception of **UIWebView** for obvious reasons) are now using **TextKit**. You can see how the core structure is now much more refined with better flow.

TextKit can be divided into three primary classes:

- `NSTextStorage`: This class is used to store all text attribute information. Think of it as an internal blueprint for all text effects. It is important to note that `NSTextStorage` is a subclass of the `NSMutableAttributedString` class, which is why it is responsible for all text attributes. In addition to storing text attributes, `NSTextStorage` will also make sure everything stays consistent during all editing operations.

- `NSLayoutManager`: This class will manage the way the data found in `NSTextStorage` is laid out in the view (as the name implies). `NSTextStorage` will notify this class if any changes or modifications have been made to the stored text attributes. It will then update the views accordingly. As a result, changes are reflected almost instantaneously.

- `NSTextContainer`: This class is responsible for specifying the view that the text will be displayed in. `NSTextContainer` also keeps track of the information related to the view, such as size/frame or shape. Most notably, `NSTextContainer` is capable of storing an array of bezier paths, which we will use later when creating exclusion paths. This is what allows TextKit to flow text around images and other objects.

TextKit can be used for multiple text-based effects. This includes responding to user-selected text sizes with dynamic type, wrapping text around an image with exclusion paths, and text formatting similar to a rich text editor.

In this chapter, we will cover all of these features in detail and then apply some of them to our application text. To start, let's look at dynamic type.

Dynamic type

One of the biggest new features of iOS 7 from a user experience standpoint is the ability to adjust OS-wide text formatting. This includes increasing the font weight (bold) and text size. These settings can be set in the device's settings application. Although it is not a requirement to support dynamic type, it is recommended to do so! Here is an example of these settings:

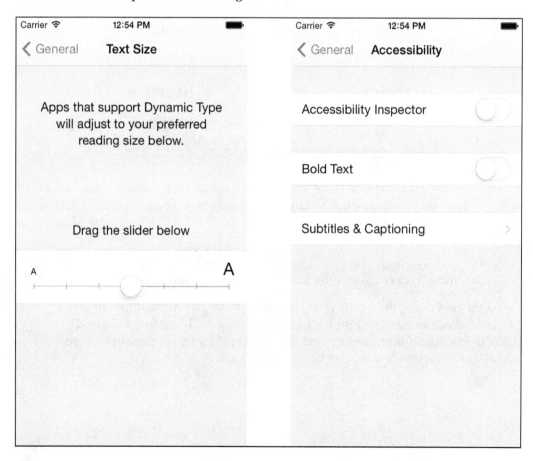

When typically dealing with fonts, we specify the font family name and the size we want to set, as follows:

```
[UIFont fontWithName:@"HelveticaNeue" size:19.0f]
```

When working with dynamic type, we will use fonts with styles instead of using the literal name of any font unlike the preceding code. UIFont has been equipped with a new method called preferredFontForTextStyle. This loads the selected font preferences from the user's device and sets the text to the given style. Here is an example of the multiple font styles:

Body	Body	**Body**
Caption 1	Caption 1	**Caption 1**
Caption 2	Caption 2	**Caption 2**
Footnote	Footnote	**Footnote**
Headline	**Headline**	**Headline**
Subhead	Subhead	**Subhead**

The text on the left-hand side is the smallest size able to be rendered, the middle text is the largest size possible, while the right-hand side text is each an option in bold format. Let's take a look at an example of using TextKit for dynamic type. Here is a code example:

```
self.foodDateLabel.font = [UIFont
    preferredFontForTextStyle:UIFontTextStyleHeadline];
```

As mentioned in the preceding code, we are not using an explicit font name, but instead are using one of the six included styles. By doing this, we avoid using hard-coded font names for our application. As a result, our application will respond very well to user-defined font selections.

Handling updates

The preceding code will automatically render based on the user settings. A problem occurs when you switch to settings and adjust the text size. If you switch back to the application without closing it first, the text updates will not be reflected. This is because in order to respond to actual changes, your controller must respond to changes made using `NSNotificatonCenter`.

By adding the following code to the end of any `viewDidLoad` method, you can have your controller respond to text updates:

```
[[NSNotificationCenter defaultCenter] addObserver:self
                                        selector:@selector(prefer
redContentSizeChanged:)
                                        name:UIContentSizeCat
egoryDidChangeNotification
                                        object:nil];
```

The defined selector will look something like this:

```
- (void)preferredContentSizeChanged:(NSNotification *)notification {
    self.textView.font = [UIFont preferredFontForTextStyle:UIFontTextS
tyleHeadline];
}
```

First we register our class to receive notification updates based on the preferred content size changing. So, if a user switches to the settings application and changes the text size, our app will intercept this and call the defined method `preferredContentSizeChanged`. Earlier, this method simply set the font; however, now it will be pulling in the new user-defined text size.

Changing the text size can also affect your view layouts. Because of this, you want to have your views to be responsive based on the text. Most of this can be done using Auto Layout. While Auto Layout may work well in most cases, one area where it does not work well is determining row height.

Exclusion paths

Exclusion paths allow you to wrap text around a particular view. Most text editors provide support for this feature, and with TextKit, you can now do it in your applications. With TextKit, you can wrap your text around both complex and simple paths. For instance, you may want to wrap your text around a simple circle or around a more complex shape such as a butterfly image. You may want to use this feature when displaying text with images, or even views that provide relevant details related to the text.

Let's assume you have a circular UIView that contains data related to a piece of text. We want to center the circular UIImageView and wrap the text around it on all sides. To test this, let's add a text view to our storyboard and wrap some filler text around our food image. Switch to **Main.Storyboard** and select the FoodDetailViewController class. Drag over a text view and resize it to be bigger than the food image. Additionally, make sure that the text view is beneath the image view. Here is what your storyboard should look like:

Make sure to create an outlet to FoodDetailViewController for our new text view. Give it the name textview.

Switch to FoodDetailViewController.m and scroll to viewDidLoad. Add this line of code at the very bottom:

```
UIBezierPath *circleExclusion = [UIBezierPath bezierPathWithOvalInRect
:CGRectMake(60, 40, 210, 210)];
    self.textView.textContainer.exclusionPaths = @[circleExclusion];
```

Here, we create a new bezier path and give it coordinates of a rectangle that are equal to those of our image view rectangle. Now that we have defined the shape for exclusion, it is time to tell the text view to pay attention to this exclusion path. TextKit has included an additional property to the text container of all text-based views called `exclusionPaths`. This parameter accepts an array, which means that multiple exclusions can be handled at once. Here is the result:

Adding letterpress

Any text can appear to be letter pressed with the right amount of shadow and highlight. TextKit provides an easy and effective way to accomplish this with a new attribute parameter called `NSTextEffectLetterpressStyle`.

Here is an example with code:

```
NSDictionary *attributes = @{ NSForegroundColorAttributeName :
   [UIColor blueColor],
NSTextEffectAttributeName : NSTextEffectLetterpressStyle};
NSAttributedString* attrString = [[NSAttributedString alloc]
                                 initWithString:someString
                                 attributes:attributes];
```

Using attributed strings, we can apply this specific text effect in addition to other attributes. That's all it takes to apply this subtle effect! Take a look at our app as an example:

Text formatting

With TextKit, we can apply some fairly simple text editing properties to our text. These include bold, italics, and underlined text. In order to do this, we are going to use a brand new class available in iOS 7, `UIFontDescriptor`. This class is used to describe a font and all of its attributes. Also, more importantly, you are able to directly modify attributes and create a new font. All font attributes are represented by either a dictionary or a key string constant.

Making text bold and italicizing

Let's take a look at a piece of code to see how we can make bold text using
`UIFontDescriptor`:

```
NSDictionary *currentAttributesDict = [self.textView.textStorage
attributesAtIndex:0

effectiveRange:nil];

UIFont *currentFont = [currentAttributesDict objectForKey:NSFontAttri
buteName];

UIFontDescriptor *fontDescriptor = [currentFont fontDescriptor];
UIFontDescriptor *changedFontDescriptor = [fontDescriptor fontDescript
orWithSymbolicTraits:UIFontDescriptorTraitBold];

UIFont *updatedFont = [UIFont fontWithDescriptor:changedFontDescriptor
size:0.0];

NSDictionary *dict = @{NSFontAttributeName: updatedFont};

    [self.textView.textStorage setAttributes:dict range:NSMakeRange(0,
self.textView.text.length)];
```

First we are grabbing the current attributes from a text view's text storage object.
Next we are creating a reference to the original font used for this piece of text. We
want to do this just in case we need that information (this is mostly dependent on
why the application is using `UIFontDescriptor`). We also create a reference to the
current font descriptor as well. Once we have all of this information, we create a new
font descriptor and set its symbolic trait to be bold. Lastly, we create an instance of
our new font that used our new font descriptor and assign it to our text view. To
change the text to italics, simply pass the proper symbolic trait.

A symbolic trait is actually just a property of a font that describes its style. It is an
unsigned 32-bit integer. Here is the list of all traits that has been provided by Apple:

```
typedef enum : uint32_t {
  /* Typeface info (lower 16 bits of
  UIFontDescriptorSymbolicTraits) */
  UIFontDescriptorTraitItalic = 1u << 0,
  UIFontDescriptorTraitBold = 1u << 1,
  UIFontDescriptorTraitExpanded = 1u << 5,
  UIFontDescriptorTraitCondensed = 1u << 6,
  UIFontDescriptorTraitMonoSpace = 1u << 10,
  UIFontDescriptorTraitVertical = 1u << 11,
  UIFontDescriptorTraitUIOptimized = 1u << 12,
```

```
    UIFontDescriptorTraitTightLeading = 1u << 15,
    UIFontDescriptorTraitLooseLeading = 1u << 16,

/* Font appearance info (upper 16 bits of
UIFontDescriptorSymbolicTraits */
    UIFontDescriptorClassMask = 0xF0000000,

    UIFontDescriptorClassUnknown = 0u << 28,
    UIFontDescriptorClassOldStyleSerifs = 1u << 28,
    UIFontDescriptorClassTransitionalSerifs = 2u << 28,
    UIFontDescriptorClassModernSerifs = 3u << 28,
    UIFontDescriptorClassClarendonSerifs = 4u << 28,
    UIFontDescriptorClassSlabSerifs = 5u << 28,
    UIFontDescriptorClassFreeformSerifs = 7u << 28,
    UIFontDescriptorClassSansSerif = 8u << 28,
    UIFontDescriptorClassOrnamentals = 9u << 28,
    UIFontDescriptorClassScripts = 10u << 28,
    UIFontDescriptorClassSymbolic = 12u << 28
} UIFontDescriptorSymbolicTraits;
```

Underlining text

Using TextKit to underline text is accomplished using a method similar to any one of the methods shown in the preceding code, with some modifications. Here is a code sample:

```
NSDictionary *currentAttributesDict = [self.textView.textStorage
attributesAtIndex:0

effectiveRange:nil];
NSDictionary *dict;

if ([currentAttributesDict
  objectForKey:NSUnderlineStyleAttributeName] ==
nil || [[currentAttributesDict objectForKey:NSUnderlineStyleAttributeN
ame] intValue] == 0) {

  dict = @{NSUnderlineStyleAttributeName:
    [NSNumber numberWithInt:1]};

}
else{
  dict = @{NSUnderlineStyleAttributeName:
    [NSNumber numberWithInt:0]};
}

[_textView.textStorage setAttributes:dict range:NSMakeRange(0,
  self.textView.text.length)];
```

Here we must check if the NSUnderlineStyleAttributeName attribute already exists in our current text attributes. From here, we simply turn the underline attribute **On** or **Off** and apply it to our text.

Summary

TextKit offers many great ways to manipulate text in iOS. Supporting these features is key to providing a better experience for users. I recommend that you take the time to navigate through Apple's documentation. We have covered many of the standard uses in this chapter. TextKit is a very powerful new API that will continue to provide innovative ways to be used.

In the final chapter, we are going to cover UIKit Dynamics. We will learn how adding physics to our UI elements can create an exciting experience!

8
Adding Physics with UIKit Dynamics

This chapter will cover the basics of how UIKit Dynamics manages your application's behaviors. We will cover specific behaviors, such as gravity, bounce, and other physics properties. Additionally, we will learn how to create physical boundaries so that our views have something to collide with. Without these boundaries, our views would continue moving forever without stopping. We will cover how our views will interact with one another, including collision detection/notifications and attaching views to one another. Lastly, we will talk about motion effects and about creating a parallax effect similar to iOS 7's home screen that moves when tilting your device. We have a lot to cover, so let's get started!

Motion and physics in UIKit

With the introduction of iOS 7, Apple completely removed the skeuomorphic design that has been used since the introduction of the iPhone and iOS. In its place is a new and refreshing flat design that features muted gradients and minimal interface elements. Apple has strongly encouraged developers to move away from a skeuomorphic and real-world-based design in favor of these flat designs.

Although we are guided away from a real-world *look*, Apple also strongly encourages that your user interface have a real-world *feel*. Some may think this is a contradiction; however, the goal is to give users a deeper connection to the user interface. UI elements that respond to touch, gestures, and changes in orientation are examples of how to apply this new design paradigm. In order to help assist in this new design approach, Apple has introduced two very nifty APIs, UIKit Dynamics and Motion Effects.

UIKit Dynamics

To put it simply, iOS 7 has a fully featured physics engine built into UIKit. You can manipulate specific properties to provide a more real-world feel to your interface. This includes gravity, springs, elasticity, bounce, and force to name a few. Each interface item will contain its own properties and the dynamic engine will abide by these properties.

Motion effects

One of the coolest features of iOS 7 on our devices is the parallax effect found on the home screen. Tilting the device in any direction will pan the background image to emphasize depth. Using motion effects, we can monitor the data supplied by the device's accelerometer to adjust our interface based on movement and orientation.

By combining these two features, you can create great looking interfaces with a realistic feel that brings it to life. To demonstrate UIKit Dynamics, we will be adding some code to our `FoodDetailViewController.m` file to create some nice effects and animations.

Adding gravity

Open `FoodDetailViewController.m` and add the following instance variables to the view controller:

```
UIDynamicAnimator* animator;
UIGravityBehavior* gravity;
```

Scroll to `viewDidLoad` and add the following code to the bottom of the method:

```
animator = [[UIDynamicAnimator alloc] initWithReferenceView:self.view];
gravity = [[UIGravityBehavior alloc] initWithItems:@[self.
foodImageView]];
    [animator addBehavior:gravity];
```

Run the application, open the **My Foods** view, select a food item from the table view, and watch what happens. The food image should start to accelerate towards the bottom of the screen until it eventually falls off the screen, as shown in the following set of screenshots:

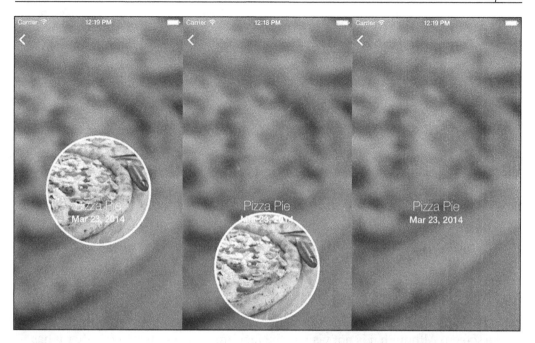

Let's go over the code, specifically the two new classes that were just introduced, `UIDynamicAnimator` and `UIGravityBehavior`.

UIDynamicAnimator

This is the core component of UIKit Dynamics. It is safe to say that the dynamic animator is the physics engine itself wrapped in a convenient and easy-to-use class. The animator will do nothing on its own, but instead keep track of behaviors assigned to it. Each behavior will interact inside of this physics engine.

UIGravityBehavior

Behaviors are the core compositions of UIKit Dynamics animation. These behaviors all define individual responses to the physics environment. This particular behavior mimics the effects of gravity by applying force. Each behavior is associated with a view (or views) when created. Because you explicitly define this property, you can control which views will perform the behavior.

Behavior properties

Almost all behaviors have multiple properties that can be adjusted to the desired effect. A good example is the gravity behavior. We can adjust its angle and magnitude. Add the following code before adding the behavior to the animator:

```
gravity.magnitude = 0.1f;
```

Run the application and test it to see what happens. The picture view will start to fall; however, this time it will be at a much slower rate. Replace the preceding code line with the following line:

```
gravity.magnitude = 10.0f;
```

Run the application, and this time you will notice that the image falls much faster. Feel free to play with these properties and get a feel for each value.

Creating boundaries

When dealing with gravity, UIKit Dynamics does not conform to the boundaries of the screen. Although it is not visible, the food image continues to fall after it has passed the edge of the screen. It will continue to fall unless we set boundaries that will contain the image view. At the top of the file, create another instance variable:

```
UICollisionBehavior *collision;
```

Now in our `viewDidLoad` method, add the following code below our gravity code:

```
collision = [[UICollisionBehavior alloc] initWithItems:@[self.
foodImageView]];
collision.translatesReferenceBoundsIntoBoundary = YES;

[animator addBehavior:collision];
```

Here we are creating an instance of a new class (which is a behavior), `UICollisionBehavior`. Just like our gravity behavior, we associate this behavior with our food image view.

Rather than explicitly defining the coordinates for the boundary, we use the convenient `translatesReferenceBoundsIntoBoundary` property on our collision behavior. By setting this property to `yes`, the boundary will be defined by the bounds of the reference view that we set when allocating our UIDynamics animator. Because the reference view is `self.view`, the boundary is now the visible space of our view.

Run the application and watch how the image will fall, but stop once it reaches the bottom of the screen, as shown in the following screenshot:

Collisions

With our image view responding to gravity and our screen bounds we can start detecting collisions. You may have noticed that when the image view is falling, it falls right through our two labels below it.

This is because UIKit Dynamics will only respond to `UIView` elements that have been assigned behaviors. Each behavior can be assigned to multiple objects, and each object can have multiple behaviors. Because our labels have no behaviors associated with them, the UIKit Dynamics physics engine simply ignores it.

Let's make the food image view collide with the date label. To do this, we simply need to add the label to the collision behavior allocation call. Here is what the new code looks like:

```
collision = [[UICollisionBehavior alloc] initWithItems:@[self.
foodImageView, self.foodDateLabel]];
```

As you can see, all we have done is add `self.foodDateLabel` to the `initWithItems` array property. As mentioned before, any single behavior can be associated with multiple items. Run your code and see what happens. When the image falls, it hits the date label but continues to fall, pushing the date label with it.

Because we didn't associate the gravity behavior with the label, it does not fall immediately. Although it does not respond to gravity, the label will still be moved because it is a physics object after all. This approach is not ideal, so let's use another awesome feature of UIKit Dynamics, invisible boundaries.

Creating invisible boundaries

We are going to take a slightly different approach to this problem. Our label is only a point of reference for where we want to add a boundary that will stop our food image view. Because of this, the label does not need to be associated with any UIKit Dynamic behaviors. Remove `self.foodDateLabel` from the following code:

```
collision = [[UICollisionBehavior alloc] initWithItems:@[self.
foodImageView, self.foodDateLabel]];
```

Instead, add the following code to the bottom of `viewDidLoad` but before we add our collision behavior to the animator:

```
// Add a boundary to the top edge
CGPoint topEdge = CGPointMake(self.foodDateLabel.frame.origin.x + self.
foodDateLabel.frame.size.width, self.foodDateLabel.frame.origin.y);
[collision addBoundaryWithIdentifier:@"barrier" fromPoint:self.
foodDateLabel.frame.origin toPoint:topEdge];
```

Here we add a boundary to the collision behavior and pass some parameters. First we define an identifier, which we will use later, and then we pass the food date label's origin as the `fromPoint` property. The `toPoint` property is set to the CGPoint we created using the food date label's frame.

Go ahead and run the application, and you will see that the food image will now stop at the invisible boundary we defined. The label is still visible to the user, but the dynamic animator ignores it. Instead the animator sees the barrier we defined and responds accordingly, even though the barrier is invisible to the user.

Here is a side-by-side comparison of the before and after:

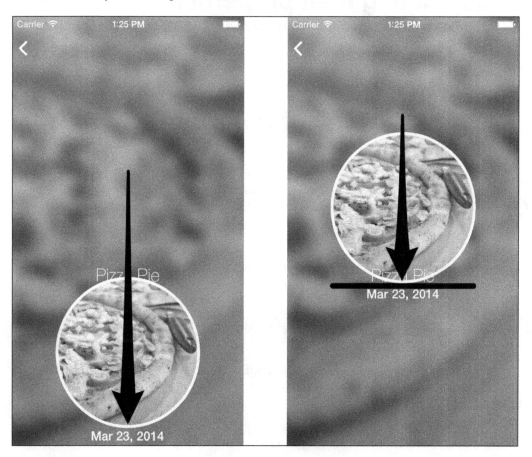

Dynamic items

When using UIKit Dynamics, it is important to understand what UIKit Dynamics items are. Rather than referencing dynamics as views, they are referenced as items, which adhere to the `UIDynamicItem` protocol. This protocol defines the center, transform, and bounds of any object that adheres to this protocol. `UIView` is the most common class that adheres to the `UIDynamicItem` protocol. Another example of a class that conforms to this protocol is the `UICollectionViewLayoutAttributes` class.

Manipulating item properties

As mentioned before, UIDynamics items have properties that can be manipulated and applied to multiple views/items in your interface. Let's see what it looks like to adjust the elasticity property and apply it to our food image view.

Scroll to `viewDidLoad` and add the following code to its end:

```
UIDynamicItemBehavior* itemBehaviour = [[UIDynamicItemBehavior alloc]
initWithItems:@[self.foodImageView]];
itemBehaviour.elasticity = 0.6;
[animator addBehavior:itemBehaviour];
```

Here, we create a `UIDynamicItemBehavior` instance and initialize it with our `self.foodImageView`. Next, we set the elasticity property and then add this new behavior to our animator. Go ahead and run your code, and watch how the food image view will now bounce a few extra times. Play with the elasticity value to see different results.

Elasticity is one of the many behaviors that can be altered. The following is a list of all the properties available with `UIDynamicItemBehavior`:

- **Elasticity**: This property will define how elastic a collision is. The best way to remember this is how bouncy the object will be. The higher the value, the more an item will bounce.

- **Friction**: If an object slides across another surface, the friction property is used to determine how much resistance the object receives.

- **Density**: This sets the overall simulated mass of the item. As with real physics, the higher the mass, the more the force required to move an item. One example of how to keep an item from moving when collided with is to give it a very high-density compared to the other items colliding with it.

- **Resistance**: This is the resistance applied to any movement, not just sliding across another surface as in the case of friction.

- **angularResistance**: When an item rotates, this property will determine the resistance to the rotation.

- **allowsRotation**: An optional property to keep an item from rotating, regardless of what collisions and forces affect it.

Collision notifications

So far, we have set up gravity and added some boundaries, including an invisible boundary for our date label. It is very common to respond to collisions by performing some sort of task. For instance, in a game, once an enemy collides with a bullet, we would destroy the enemy and increase the score.

We can track collisions by using collision notifications. In order to do so, we must have our class adopt `UICollisionBehaviorDelegate`. Switch to `FoodDetailViewController.h` and add the following protocol:

```
@interface FoodDetailViewController : UIViewController
  <UICollisionBehaviorDelegate>
```

Now switch back to `FoodDetailViewController.m` and locate the code we wrote to create the collision behavior. Add the following line of code:

```
collision.collisionDelegate = self;
```

By setting the collision delegate, we can now use the following delegate method:

```
- (void)collisionBehavior:(UICollisionBehavior *)behavior
  beganContactForItem:(id<UIDynamicItem>)item
  withBoundaryIdentifier:(id<NSCopying>)identifier
  atPoint:(CGPoint)p {

    NSLog(@"Boundary contact occurred - %@", identifier);

}
```

This delegate method gets called every time a collision occurs, and we have set it up to output the collision identifier we defined earlier. Run the code, and your console output should look as follows:

```
▼  ▶  ‖  ⟳  ↓  ↑  ✦  | No Selection
2014-03-23 14:16:44.231 Food and Me[1310:60b] Boundary contact occurred - barrier
2014-03-23 14:16:44.615 Food and Me[1310:60b] Boundary contact occurred - barrier
2014-03-23 14:16:44.848 Food and Me[1310:60b] Boundary contact occurred - barrier
2014-03-23 14:16:44.998 Food and Me[1310:60b] Boundary contact occurred - barrier
```

Using a combination of identifiers and other properties passed to this delegate method, we can detect which collisions are happening and respond accordingly. For example, let's animate the alpha of the food image view when a collision occurs. Replace your delegate method code with the following code:

```
- (void)collisionBehavior:(UICollisionBehavior *)behavior
  beganContactForItem:(id<UIDynamicItem>)item
  withBoundaryIdentifier:(id<NSCopying>)identifier
  atPoint:(CGPoint)p {

    if ([(NSString *)identifier isEqualToString:@"barrier"]) {
        // The barrier was collided with
        [UIView animateWithDuration:0.3f animations:^{

            self.foodImageView.alpha = 0.0f;

        }];
    }

}
```

Here we cast the identifier as an NSString and then check if it is equal to the collision identifier we want. If so, we perform a simple UIView animation that sets the alpha value of the image view to zero, thus making it invisible. Using this delegate method properly will allow you to accomplish a large number of tasks based on collisions.

Attaching items to other items

In addition to gravity and other physics properties, UIKit Dynamics also allows your physics objects to interact with one another as they would in the real physical world. For example, we can use the UIAttachmentBehavior method to link items together as if they are attached with an invisible brace. Let's have our application create a new square view and then attach it to our food image view, but only when a collision occurs. Because our food image view will bounce a couple of times, the collision will be detected each time. To keep from creating multiple squares, let's create another instance variable to keep track of the first bounce.

Add the following line of code in the implementation block in FoodDetailViewController.m:

```
BOOL firstBounce;
```

Now replace our delegate method code with the following code:

```
- (void)collisionBehavior:(UICollisionBehavior *)behavior
beganContactForItem:(id<UIDynamicItem>)item
withBoundaryIdentifier:(id<NSCopying>)identifier
atPoint:(CGPoint)p {

    if (!firstBounce) {

        firstBounce = YES;

        UIView* square = [[UIView alloc]
initWithFrame:CGRectMake(self.view.bounds.size.width / 2 - 50,
400, 100, 100)];
        square.backgroundColor = [UIColor greenColor];
        [self.view addSubview:square];

        [collision addItem:square];
        [gravity addItem:square];

        UIAttachmentBehavior* attach = [[UIAttachmentBehavior
alloc] initWithItem:self.foodImageView attachedToItem:square];
        [animator addBehavior:attach];

    }

}
```

Here we detect if the `firstBounce` Boolean value is not `YES`, and then create a new `UIView`, add the gravity and collision items to it, use the `UIAttachmentBehavior` method, and attach this new view to our food image view. Run the application, and you will see that on the first bounce, a green square is created. Because we attach this new view to the food image view, you will see that as it bounces the second and third times, the square view moves with it as if attached.

Snapping items

Our last behavior we will cover in this book is the `UISnapBehavior` class. UIKit Dynamics provides a built-in behavior that will snap an item from its starting point to a specified end point with built-in damping. Let's have our food image view snap from the top of the screen into its final position.

Scroll to `viewDidLoad` and remove all of our gravity and collision code (keep our animator). Add the following code to `viewDidLoad`:

```
UISnapBehavior *snapBehaviour = [[UISnapBehavior alloc]
    initWithItem:self.foodImageView snapToPoint:CGPointMake(160,
    202)];
snapBehaviour.damping = 0.65f;
[animator addBehavior:snapBehaviour];
```

Here we allocate new `UISnapBehavior` and `init` options with our food image view. We also pass the point we want the item to snap to, in this case, the final position of the image view. We set the damping value to be a bit higher to give a milder spring effect (the lower the number, the more springy the item will be).

The last thing to do is to change the starting point of the food image view. Switch to **Main.storyboard** and drag the food image view to the top of the screen as high as you wish (even offscreen). It is important to note that the greater the distance of the starting point to the end point, the more springy the snap, so take this into consideration when setting the `damping` property.

Run our application and see the results. The food image view should snap into place with a nice spring effect. As you can see, using UIKit Dynamics is not only simple, but can be very powerful.

Using motion in our app

In addition to UIKit Dynamics, we can also use `UIMotionEffects` to adjust the user interface when a device is tilted horizontally. `UIMotionEffects` is an abstract class that works best when subclassed. Apple has already made a subclass of `UIMotionEffects` that will cover almost all use cases of motion in your apps. This subclass is the `UIInterpolatingMotionEffect` class.

The `UIInterpolatingMotionEffect` instance is initialized with a key path and a type. The type is what defines vertical and horizontal motions. The class will automatically set the key value path based on the device's movements.

In our `viewDidLoad` method, add the following code at the bottom:

```
UIInterpolatingMotionEffect *horizontalMotionEffect =
    [[UIInterpolatingMotionEffect alloc] initWithKeyPath:@"center.x"
    type:UIInterpolatingMotionEffectTypeTiltAlongHorizontalAxis];

horizontalMotionEffect.minimumRelativeValue = @(-30);
```

```
horizontalMotionEffect.maximumRelativeValue = @(30);

[self.foodImageView addMotionEffect:horizontalMotionEffect];
[self.foodNameLabel addMotionEffect:horizontalMotionEffect];
[self.foodDateLabel addMotionEffect:horizontalMotionEffect];
```

Here we create our `UIInterpolatingMotionEffect` instance and assign it to the horizontal axis motion tracking. Next we set a minimum and maximum relative value. This determines how much the items will move left and right to simulate the parallax effect we want. Lastly, we add the motion effect to all views that we want. Our `keyPath` value can be assigned to a number of different values for different effects. Run the application on a device and select a food item's detailed view to see the results!

Additionally, we can go further by grouping multiple motion effects together, such as both vertical and horizontal motions. Replace the preceding code with the following:

```
UIInterpolatingMotionEffect *horizontalMotionEffect =
    [[UIInterpolatingMotionEffect alloc] initWithKeyPath:@"center.x"
    type:UIInterpolatingMotionEffectTypeTiltAlongHorizontalAxis];

    horizontalMotionEffect.minimumRelativeValue = @(-30);
    horizontalMotionEffect.maximumRelativeValue = @(30);

    UIInterpolatingMotionEffect *verticalMotionEffect =
    [[UIInterpolatingMotionEffect alloc] initWithKeyPath:@"center.y"
    type:UIInterpolatingMotionEffectTypeTiltAlongVerticalAxis];

    verticalMotionEffect.minimumRelativeValue = @(-30);
    verticalMotionEffect.maximumRelativeValue = @(30);

    UIMotionEffectGroup *group = [UIMotionEffectGroup new];

    group.motionEffects = @[horizontalMotionEffect,
    verticalMotionEffect];

    [self.foodImageView addMotionEffect:group];
    [self.foodNameLabel addMotionEffect:group];
    [self.foodDateLabel addMotionEffect:group];
```

Here we simply duplicate the horizontal motion effect, but we set `keyPath` to `center.y` and `type` to `vertical`. Run the application and check out the results.

As great and easy as these effects are, be careful not to go overboard. Each of the items discussed in this chapter is designed to add subtle effects that work together for an overall better user experience.

Summary

We have done it! From start to finish, we have built a fully functional application using many of the great new features of iOS 7 and Xcode 5. In this chapter, we topped everything off by adding some cool physical properties to our views. Stacking these behaviors and motion effects together can create some really unique interface effects. Now that we are at the conclusion of this book, you should be very comfortable stepping into iOS 7 development. Taking advantage of all the new features is the first step to building better applications with a better experience!

Index

Symbols

A

B

C

D

Thank you for buying
Application Development in iOS 7

About Packt Publishing

Packt, pronounced 'packed', published its first book *"Mastering phpMyAdmin for Effective MySQL Management"* in April 2004 and subsequently continued to specialize in publishing highly focused books on specific technologies and solutions.

Our books and publications share the experiences of your fellow IT professionals in adapting and customizing today's systems, applications, and frameworks. Our solution based books give you the knowledge and power to customize the software and technologies you're using to get the job done. Packt books are more specific and less general than the IT books you have seen in the past. Our unique business model allows us to bring you more focused information, giving you more of what you need to know, and less of what you don't.

Packt is a modern, yet unique publishing company, which focuses on producing quality, cutting-edge books for communities of developers, administrators, and newbies alike. For more information, please visit our website: www.packtpub.com.

Writing for Packt

We welcome all inquiries from people who are interested in authoring. Book proposals should be sent to author@packtpub.com. If your book idea is still at an early stage and you would like to discuss it first before writing a formal book proposal, contact us; one of our commissioning editors will get in touch with you.

We're not just looking for published authors; if you have strong technical skills but no writing experience, our experienced editors can help you develop a writing career, or simply get some additional reward for your expertise.

Application Development with Parse using iOS SDK

ISBN: 978-1-78355-033-3   Paperback: 112 pages

Develop the backend of your applications instantly using Parse iOS SDK

1. Build your applications using Parse iOS which serves as a complete cloud-based backend service.

2. Understand and write your code on cloud to minimize the load on the client side.

3. Learn how to create your own applications using Parse SDK, with the help of the step-by-step, practical tutorials.

iOS 7 Game Development

ISBN: 978-1-78355-157-6   Paperback: 120 pages

Develop powerful, engaging games with ready-to-use utilities from Sprite Kit

1. Pen your own endless runner game using Apple's new Sprite Kit framework.

2. Enhance your user experience with easy-to-use animations and particle effects using Xcode 5.

3. Utilize particle systems and create custom particle effects.

Please check **www.PacktPub.com** for information on our titles

iOS and OS X Network Programming Cookbook

ISBN: 978-1-84969-808-5   Paperback: 300 pages

Over 50 recipes to develop network applications in both the iOS and OS X environment

1. Use several Apple and third-party APIs to develop both server and client networked applications.

2. Shows you how to integrate all of the third-party libraries and APIs with your applications.

3. Includes sample projects for both iOS and OS X environments.

RestKit for iOS

ISBN: 978-1-78216-370-1   Paperback: 118 pages

Link your apps and web services using RestKit

1. A step-by-step guide that goes beyond theory and into practice.

2. Learn how to overcome hurdles that might pop up along the way when using RestKit.

3. Learn how to integrate new frameworks into an existing app.